MUSLIM MANNERS

*A Guide for
Parents and Teachers of
Muslim Children*

Iqbal Ahmad Azami

UK ISLAMIC ACADEMY

Revised Edition

ISBN 1 872531 67 9

Published by
UK Islamic Academy
P.O. Box 6645
Leicester LE5 5WT
United Kingdom

Website: www.ukiabooks.com
E-mail: info@ukiabooks.com

British Library Cataloguing-in-Publication Data
A catalogue record for this book is available from the British Library.

Design and typeset by: Muhammad al-Madani

Printed and bound in the UK by: Deluxe Printers

Contents

قَالَ عَلَيْهِ الصَّلَاةُ وَالسَّلَامُ :

إِنَّمَا بُعِثْتُ لِأُتَمِّمَ مَكَارِمَ الْأَخْلَاقِ

The Prophet ﷺ said:
'I was sent to perfect good character.'

بِسْمِ اللهِ الرَّحْمنِ الرَّحِيمِ

Foreword

Young Muslims growing up in the West are denied the constant reminders of their Creator that are observed in Muslim countries. It is difficult for them to believe that 'God Willing' used to preface people's actions in Britain before the country was secularized, just as '*Insha Allah*', with exactly the same meaning, is used by Muslims today.

Those who believe in Allah cannot ignore His influence on their daily lives. When believers find themselves surrounded by strong secular influences, however, their traditional religious customs and traditions are likely to be eroded.

Muslim Manners has been published to help counter that erosion. It provides a comprehensive guide to traditional Islamic teaching and its effect on Muslims' daily lives. Only by following Allah's guidance can Muslims live in peace while they are on earth and attain Paradise in the After-life. It is through a strong network of Islamic attitudes and actions based on knowledge that Muslims are able to bind both to one another and to their faith. *Muslim Manners* makes a rich contribution to that necessary knowledge.

In order to live by Allah's unchanging standards Muslims need a clear understanding that Islam is a total system. This book provides information on kindness, obedience, helping others, respect, hospitality, dress and hygiene. It also covers such subjects of topical relevance to today's young Muslims growing up in the West as obligations to parents, choosing the right company and animal welfare.

The Editor has relied for his sources on the Holy Qur'an, the *Hadith* and traditional authorities. Although the book is aimed at 11-14 year olds, adults will also benefit from it. Parents and teachers of younger children will find it a useful source of reference while trying to strengthen positive attitudes towards Islamically-orientated behaviour. Exercises provided at the end of each chapter will help to ensure that young people fully understand the Islamic teaching on each subject.

My thanks are due to Brother Jamil Qureshi, Sister Maryam Davies, my daughters Su'ad, Shifa' and my other children for their help in producing this book. May Allah ﷻ bless them all and accept this humble effort and make it beneficial to all.

Leicester, United Kingdom   **Iqbal Ahmad Azami**
Rabī' al-Awwal, 1424

- 1 -

The Basis of Muslim Manners

Islam offers every Muslim contentment and peace of mind in his everyday living, in his relations with himself and in his relations with others. So that this peace of mind and contentment may be a serious and noble hope in a Muslim's life, Islam puts a condition on this offer. The condition is that the Muslim must love Allah ﷻ and express that love in his actions, by following Allah's law. But that, without love of Allah ﷻ, is an uphill task and, in the end, not possible. How then does this love come about, what is it, and what particular actions express it?

If we are asked whom we love best, we should most probably answer, those we loved first, our parents. The reasons are not difficult to find. We grow up from being helpless to being independent in the shelter of their affection. It is our parents who feed and clothe us, who try to share and solve our problems. It is only when we are older, perhaps, that we begin to realize how much we needed them, how much they gave up for our sake, because of their love for us.

Yet, as much as they did, it is only a very small part of the blessings of Allah ﷻ Who created all things. Born powerless, we would certainly die without motherly love and fatherly protection. It is Allah ﷻ who put love for us in our parents' hearts. It is Allah ﷻ who created the world into which we are born, and created it for us so that it suits us. Air and light, a day to work in and make use of the earth's riches, its food, its minerals, its energies, its varied loveliness of form and colour; and then the night to rest from the day. No-one is better than Allah ﷻ in providing for us; no-one is better than Allah ﷻ in protecting us from the terrors of the earth. In crisis it is to Allah ﷻ we call for help. There are indeed times of fear in every human life, created by Allah ﷻ also, just so that we may learn to turn to Him. When all is said and done, it is to Allah ﷻ that we owe our deepest thanks, and it is to Him that all living things return.

The love of our parents, great as it is, is small compared to the love Allah ﷻ shows to His creatures. If we mis-behave, our parents may scold or punish us. But how often man disobeys Allah ﷻ! He could if He wished destroy the whole creation in an instant, but He tolerates all man's acts of disobedience and blesses His servants, giving them time to do better. Instead of punishing us, He shows us caring patience, because He is the Most Forgiving and His blessings surpass His anger. His love and affection are unlimited, while the mistakes man makes and all man's sinning are, by the mercy of Allah ﷻ, quite limited.

Once, one of the Companions of the Prophet Muhammad ﷺ, when passing by a tree, heard the chirping of tiny birds in a nest. He placed a sheet over the nest to catch the nestlings as they tried to leave the nest. The mother bird, anxious for the safety of her nestlings, came too close and was also caught. The Companion then took the birds and placed them on the ground at the feet of the Blessed Prophet 鷖. But to everyone's surprise, instead of flying away, and at the risk of her own life the mother bird stayed to protect the nestlings. The Blessed Prophet 鷖 then said to the Companion: 'You are surprised to see how the bird behaves to protect her young ones. By the name of the One who sent me with the message of Truth, I swear that Allah 鷖 is more kind and affectionate to His servants.' Then he advised the Companion to return the birds to their nest, and said: 'The affection and kindness of Allah 鷖 can be measured from the fact that He has given only a hundredth part of His love and affection to His creatures and has kept the rest with Him and it will be clearly seen on the Day of Judgement.'

Proof of Allah's mercy and love is everywhere visible in the world; it is visible too in our relations with others: in the fact that we have family life, parents, brothers, sisters, cousins, and friends; and in the course of time, we start families of our own, and enjoy the blessings of being parents. Nevertheless, despite all this, men and women are tempted away from the love they owe to Allah 鷖. As the Qur'an tells us:

$$ \text{وَمِنَ ٱلنَّاسِ مَن يَتَّخِذُ مِن دُونِ ٱللَّهِ أَندَادًا يُحِبُّونَهُمْ كَحُبِّ ٱللَّهِ وَٱلَّذِينَ ءَامَنُوٓاْ أَشَدُّ حُبًّا لِّلَّهِ ... ١٦٥} $$

Yet there are men who take others apart from Allah (and worship them) as equals (to Allah 鷖); they love them in the way that they should love (only)

Allah. But those who have Faith are overflowing in their love for Allah. [al-Baqarah 2: 165]

We say that we love our parents. But what does this love demand from us, how should this love be shown in our behaviour? Of course by loving them in return, and those who are dear to them, and by acting according to their wishes. Thus, we should love our brothers and sisters who are dear to our parents, and our parents' friends who are also dear to them. We should approve of the way they dress, we should look after their house, property and other belongings, and remember their kindnesses. We should also favour their habits and ways of doing things, and dislike any rudeness or insult to them. And if we do not do these things, our love is not really acted out and could therefore be rejected as false.

In the same way, when someone says that he loves Allah ﷻ above all, he must love what Allah ﷻ loves and turn from what He turns from. Friends of Allah ﷻ should be his friends and Allah's enemies his enemies. Thus, we must like and dislike in keeping with the commands of Allah ﷻ and not just to please our own likes and fancies. The only measure of the truth of our love for Allah ﷻ is that we try to act on His commands. We can do this through love and affection for the Blessed Prophet Muhammad ﷺ who was the most favoured of Allah's Messengers, the noblest and most comprehensive in his character. We must try to pattern our actions on those of the Blessed Prophet Muhammad ﷺ and his Companions. It is our duty to serve our parents, elders and teachers because Allah ﷻ has commanded us to do so. If one of them defies Allah ﷻ and disobeys Him, then we must not follow his lead; rather, we should treat him well for his favours to us and try, with polite and kind words, to guide him to the right path.

Love of Allah ﷻ can be expressed directly in acts of worship. It is indeed a test of our love if we give up our sleep to rise early in the morning and do *wudu* in readiness for prayers at the mosque alongside other Muslims. And it is a hard test too when we endure hunger and thirst in the month of fasting, especially where the climate is hot or where the day is long. But our love of Allah ﷻ cannot be proved by doing only these things. The harder tests come when there is a choice of what to do, a choice between popular custom and the verdict of *Shari'ah* or Allah's Law.

For example, in business dealings our personal interest may suffer if we follow Allah's Law instead of popular custom. Of course, if we disregard the commands of *Shari'ah*, it means that we have let ourselves fail the test. Real success lies in giving up our own interests and obeying Allah's Law without any laziness or unwilling-ness or regret inside. Only then can we be sure that we have been equal to the test, for then we have positively chosen the way of the Qur'an and the example of the Blessed Prophet ﷺ, his *Sunnah*:

فَلَا وَرَبِّكَ لَا يُؤْمِنُونَ حَتَّىٰ يُحَكِّمُوكَ فِيمَا شَجَرَ بَيْنَهُمْ ثُمَّ لَا يَجِدُواْ فِىٓ أَنفُسِهِمْ حَرَجًا مِّمَّا قَضَيْتَ وَيُسَلِّمُواْ تَسْلِيمًا ﴿٦٥﴾

But no, by your Lord! They will not be believers till they make you the judge regarding the disagree-ment between them; then they will find nothing inside themselves resisting against your verdict, but

will surrender in full submission (be fully Muslim).
[al-Nisa' 4: 65]

A yet more difficult test is when a Muslim thinks a certain
action is a religious one and intends by it to please Allah ﷻ
and His Messenger ﷺ, but then learns that this action is
not according to the command of Allah ﷻ or the example
of His Messenger ﷺ. If he then goes on in that action it
means that he is obeying himself and rejecting Allah ﷻ,
a most terrible sin. The Qur'an describes this as a form of
self-worship:

أَفَرَءَيْتَ مَنِ ٱتَّخَذَ إِلَٰهَهُ هَوَىٰهُ وَأَضَلَّهُ ٱللَّهُ عَلَىٰ عِلْمٍ وَخَتَمَ عَلَىٰ سَمْعِهِۦ وَقَلْبِهِۦ وَجَعَلَ عَلَىٰ بَصَرِهِۦ
غِشَٰوَةً فَمَن يَهْدِيهِ مِنۢ بَعْدِ ٱللَّهِ أَفَلَا تَذَكَّرُونَ ﴿٢٣﴾

*Have you taken note of him who makes his desire
his Allah, and Allah sends him the wrong way
purposely, and seals up his hearing and his heart,
and puts a covering over his sight? Then who can
lead him after Allah (has let him go the wrong way)?
Will you not then take care?* [al-Jathiyah 45: 23]

The Blessed Prophet ﷺ said: '*A perfect believer is one
whose heart likes the teachings of Allah ﷻ and His
Messenger ﷺ.*'

That is the proper goal of every Muslim, young or old, to
choose the Qur'an and *Sunnah* as the best guide in all
the choices of his life. Then, whatever he is busy doing,
he keeps Allah ﷻ in mind at all times. In this little book
we have tried to give examples of, and explain in simple,
direct words, some of those everyday Muslim choices.

Questions

1. How do we know that Allah ﷻ loves His servants?
2. Whom should the true believer most love?
3. What are the demands of love for Allah ﷻ?
4. What should be the test of friendship for a believer?
5. How can it be known that we love Allah ﷻ and His Messenger ﷺ?
6. When is a Muslim's love for the Blessed Prophet ﷺ put to the hardest test?
7. Who is a perfect believer according to the Prophet Muhammad ﷺ?

– 2 –

The Importance of
Muslim Manners

Taken together, those everyday Muslim choices can be called the rules of how to be a Muslim, or *Muslim manners*. The basic rule behind all the others is to be humble about oneself and positively considerate towards others. All religions recommend this attitude, this way of thinking about others and acting toward others: no religion has ever recommended stealing or being cruel to parents, etc. This means that a Muslim who observes these manners should not think he is being strange, or even that he will appear strange to others. Quite the opposite, he will be honoured for it, even by non-Muslims, and valued as a modest, courteous, unselfish human being. But Muslim manners are different, in two important ways.

First, Muslim manners are manners for everybody; rich, poor, male, female, young, old, everybody without exception. In most cultures of the world when people talk about manners, they mean 'fancy' or 'posh' ways of doing things, 'etiquette', the behaviour of royal courtiers to others of their own social class. Even in present-day England, for example, when people describe someone as 'well-mannered', they are more or less saying that he or she is 'posh' or 'upper class'. By contrast, a poor Muslim villager will, if he is purposefully following the example of the Blessed Prophet ﷺ, welcome a guest into his home with the same light ceremonies as the richest Muslim in the city-world of some place like New York, provided that he too, in spite of his wealth and where he lives, is purposefully following the example of the Blessed Prophet ﷺ.

Second, Muslim manners are valid for all times, as well as all places, they do not change as fashions change. In present-day England, or indeed any rich, modern society, it is the fashion for young people to say to their parents, 'Don't tell me what to do; I have my own life to lead; you go your way, I'm going mine', etc. Whether the parents agree with their children or do not agree with them, this attitude is a selfish one and can have no part in Muslim manners.

Some people argue that times have changed; it is no longer necessary for young people to depend on their parents, they can afford to start their own separate families in their own separate houses. The age of the three-generation family, when parents, grandparents and children lived in the same place, has gone for good, people argue; now we must accept the smaller family as the basic unit. But how small is small?

Because the feelings behind this change are selfish, its effect has not been to transform the family but to destroy it: more couples remain childless, on purpose, for longer; at the same time, there are more divorces so that families split up long before the children have grown up, and there are more single-parent 'families'. Within the family, whatever its size, there are more differences of taste and behaviour so that the children are often closer to their friends than to other members of their family, and they often learn more from the television than they learn from their parents. But so what, some people would argue, what if the family breaks up?

In Islam, the family is valued as something that we cannot manage without. Why? Because it is the only proper training ground that allows human beings to grow up as human beings. The most strikingly human quality of human beings is their ability to manage with each other, to give and take, to have (most of the time) kindly feelings towards each other whatever might happen on any one occasion. For example, brothers and sisters often quarrel but they just as often make up and stay brother and sister.

Within the privacy and safety of family-life people learn to adapt to each other, to forgive mistakes, to be trusting, to talk sometimes, to be silent at others, sometimes to butt-in, sometimes to leave well alone, and so on. No government, however well-intentioned, no school, how-ever good or hard working its teachers, can replace the family in this respect. That is why Islam puts such stress on loving and serving one's parents, even in preference to loving and serving one's children; why there are so many rules to improve and strengthen the privacy of family life.

Without the family, the emotional life of the individual is made so ugly and hard-hearted by selfishness that, in the end, he finds himself saying and (what is worse) believing that nobody needs him and he does not need anybody, nobody values him for his own sake and he does not value anybody either. A miserable end.

Muslim manners do not change with fashion, they have nothing to do with it. The great value of this for the Muslim community is that Muslims the world over can feel comfortable with each other. Their manners come out of a shared belief in the Qur'an and the example of the Blessed Prophet ﷺ, and this keeps them together, in the same sort of way that a family is kept together by sharing the same habits or the same accent when they speak.

The rules of Muslim manners are not a hard or harsh burden on the individual. They are a light but strong network of attitudes and actions that bind Muslims to each other and to Islam.

Most readers will know *the events of the Hijrah, the migration of the Blessed Prophet ﷺ in the company of his close friend and ally, Abu Bakr Siddiq. They were pursued by people from Makkah, anxious to catch them and put them to death. They hid in a cave. Their pursuers came right up to the mouth of the cave so that they could be clearly heard from inside. But, by the grace of Allah ﷻ, a spider had worked a web right across the mouth of the cave. Seeing it, the pursuers believed that no-one could have entered that cave, since, if they had, the spider's web would have been broken. Never has so humble a thing as a spider's web served so noble a purpose as it did on that occasion, protecting Allah's Messenger.*

Muslim manners are just like the work of that spider, a light, delicate web, protecting the Muslim community from its pursuers and enemies. Some Muslims, perhaps because they are too anxious for the security of their way of life, are very strict in insisting that such-and-such must be done in such-and-such a way *whatever the circumstances*. But this is most probably an unwise attitude. One of the most insisted-upon rules of Muslim manners is that you do not make fun of others, you do not try to make them look or feel small. If you think they are doing something wrong, you take them aside and speak to them gently. Then, if they give an explanation for why they did what they did, you trust them, accept the explanation, and forgive them. What keeps Muslim manners light is also what keeps them strong and lasting: they are patterned on the advice and example of the Blessed Prophet Muhammad ﷺ, who was not sent as a punishment but as a kindness for all the worlds.

Why is it that, unlike other religions and cultures of the world, Muslim manners remain so constant, so recognizably Muslim, from Morocco to Malaya? The answer is that from the beginning Muslim manners have been practised as a part of Muslim worship.

The majority of human beings are not able, in the ordinary conditions of life, to sacrifice everything for Allah ﷻ. Because they are not able to do that, many start to cut themselves off from prayer and then from all religious practice, and then may (in the worst case) start to reject religion altogether. In many parts of the world there is a split between the people who are 'truly' and 'fully' religious, people who live in a very controlled way in very controlled and narrow surroundings, for example monks in a monastery, nuns in a convent, and ordinary people who are not 'truly', not 'fully' religious. Then, there is often a split between ordinary days and holy days, or one holy day and the rest of the week; and there is likewise a split between 'ordinary' actions (like eating and drinking, enjoying family life, earning a living, etc.) and 'religious' actions (like praying, giving your money to the poor, comforting the sick, etc.).

Now Islam does not recognize this kind of division, and does not approve of it. It is easy to imagine the feelings of a man who hears from a monk that he must give up his worldly goods, when the man needs his worldly goods to feed his children with, while the monk has no such need. In Islam, every act, however small it is, even if it is an act that gives you immediate happiness (like eating and drinking), can be a truly religious act if it is done with the intention of pleasing Allah ﷻ and being thankful to Him.

This means that a Muslim need never feel cut off from his religion. A rich person may be able to give a great part of his wealth away and benefit many others. If he does so for Allah's sake and not so that others will praise him, then he may rightly hope that Allah ﷻ will be pleased with him. A person who is so poor that he has nothing to give away can also earn Allah's pleasure: he may see a piece of broken glass on the road and remove it, hoping to prevent some creature of Allah ﷻ suffering an injury. He can say to himself: 'In this, I have done as Allah's Messenger, peace be upon him, asked me to do.' And if there is no road, no piece of glass? In this case he can, the next time he puts on his shoes, check that no insect or animal has lodged in them, and then put on first his right shoe, then his left, and say: 'In this, I have done as the Messenger of Allah, peace be upon him, used to do.' Even though he is very poor, the man's heart is lifted and cheered and contented, because he knows he has acted positively as a Muslim should act.

In this way, the Muslim is able to be constantly mindful of being a Muslim, of his debt to Allah ﷻ, and to His Messenger ﷺ. Yet it is hard to imagine a smaller or lighter task than putting on one's shoes. Because a Muslim is kept in touch, through Muslim manners, with his religion, acts of formal prayer when worship is more concentrated, are much easier, and a more natural part of everyday life.

Questions

1. In what ways are Muslim manners different from any others?
2. What are the basic rules of Muslim manners?
3. Why is family-life so highly valued in Islam?
4. Why are Muslim manners a part of worship?
5. How should children treat their parents?
6. How do Muslim manners help to unite the Muslim community?
7. Explain how Muslim manners compare to the spider's web in protecting the Muslims?
8. Are Muslim manners hard and difficult?
9. If you see someone doing wrong, how should you deal with him or her?
10. Why do Muslim manners stay constant and unchanged?
11. In what ways do Muslim manners help Muslims to stay close to Islam?

-3-

Human Kindness

When a flower blooms, its colour and scent first touch the garden near it, and then spread. In the same way, a Muslim's acts of human kindness should first touch those nearest to him, his family and his neighbours.

Parents

In the family, parents deserve our love first. We should obey and respect them and treat them well. Even if they should do something wrong, we should look after them and try to lighten their cares and worries. Whatever we own, we should think of it as a gift from them or a result of their prayers for us. We should try to earn their blessings for our happiness in this life and the life to come.

The prayers of parents are a great blessing for their children. *The Blessed Prophet ﷺ said that when an obedient child looks with love at his parents, he gets a reward equal to that of going on a pilgrimage. Once, a Companion came to the Blessed Prophet ﷺ to ask his permission to take part in war for the sake of Allah ﷻ*

(jihad). However, when the Blessed Prophet ﷺ found out that the Companion's mother was still alive, he advised him to look after her and said that this amounted to taking part in war for the sake of Allah ﷻ.

The Blessed Prophet ﷺ also said: 'No-one is more un-fortunate than the person who has parents but cannot gain entry to heaven through serving them.' He said that people often prefer their children to their parents, but it should be the other way round. The parents' rights have been made more important in Islam, so a Muslim should prefer his parents to his children. The Blessed Prophet ﷺ also said that a man is the wealth of his parents and whatever he has in the world is really owed to them and, therefore, he should always admit this openly. He urged us never to misbehave towards parents and to talk softly when replying to them. Allah ﷻ has forbidden using harsh words to parents or putting on an 'I don't care about them' attitude.

The Blessed Prophet ﷺ urged us, after our parents' death, to pray to Allah ﷻ for their forgiveness. And to do so after reciting the Qur'an and other good deeds, so as to convey reward to them. He also asked us to pay our parents' debts and to think it our duty to respect and be of service to their friends.

Anas, ﷜ reported Allah's Messenger ﷺ as saying, 'When the parents of a man die, or one of them dies, and he has been dutiful to them, and he keeps on making supp-lications and asking forgiveness for them till Allah records that he is dutiful.'

Once, 'Abdullah, son of 'Umar al-Faruq, may Allah be pleased with both of them, was on the pilgrimage when he met a villager whom he recognized. He got down from his horse and mounted the villager in his place and he put his own headscarf on the villager's head. His companions were very surprised at this; one of them pointed out that it was a hot day, that the way was rocky, that hot winds were blowing and that he was not used to walking. By contrast, the man went on, the villagers were used to making long trips on foot, and that he should not, therefore, either have dismounted from his horse or given his headscarf to the villager. 'Abdullah ibn 'Umar ﷺ replied: 'The father of this villager was a friend of my father's and it was, therefore, necessary for me to show courtesy to him. The Blessed Prophet ﷺ has said: "The best deed is to treat friends of your father well" and, therefore, I did not think it right to watch him walking while I was riding or that he should be bare-headed in the hot sun.'

'Abdullah ibn 'Umar ﷺ showed such courtesy to a friend of his father's because the Qur'an and the advice of the Blessed Prophet ﷺ were first in his heart and mind, and not his own need or the customs and practices of others. So important is love of one's parents that the Qur'an links it with believing in the oneness of Allah ﷻ. Muslims must believe in the One Allah ﷻ and offer thanks and praise to Him; after that, they must treat their parents with kindness and offer thanks and praise to them:

﴿ وَقَضَىٰ رَبُّكَ أَلَّا تَعْبُدُوٓا۟ إِلَّآ إِيَّاهُ وَبِٱلْوَٰلِدَيْنِ إِحْسَٰنًا ۚ إِمَّا يَبْلُغَنَّ عِندَكَ ٱلْكِبَرَ أَحَدُهُمَآ أَوْ كِلَاهُمَا فَلَا تَقُل لَّهُمَآ أُفٍّ وَلَا تَنْهَرْهُمَا وَقُل لَّهُمَا قَوْلًا كَرِيمًا ﴿٢٣﴾

*Your Lord has commanded that you worship no-
one but Him and that you be kind to parents.
Whether one or both of them reaches old age in
your life-time, do not say a single word of hurt to
them, nor push them away. Rather, speak to them
in honourable words.* [al-Isra' 17: 23]

Even if a Muslim's parents have not embraced Islam, his
duties to them are still binding. Of course, the rights of
Allah ﷻ are supreme, therefore he should not abandon
religion at the request of his parents or do unlawful
things. But in all the ordinary ways, he should show them
the respect they deserve as parents.

It is also necessary to respect the elders of others if we
wish them, in turn, to respect ours. We should not do
anything that may push others into insulting our parents.
*The Blessed Prophet ﷺ said: 'One of the worst sins is to
curse one's parents.' The Companions, not understanding,
asked: 'O Messenger of Allah, who would be such a sinner
as to curse his parents?' He replied: 'He may not abuse
them himself but if he abuses the parents of some other
person who in return abuses his, it means that he himself
has abused them.'*

Mother

*A man came to the Blessed Prophet ﷺ and asked: 'O
Messenger of Allah! Whom should I serve?' The Blessed
Prophet ﷺ replied: 'You should look after your mother.'
The man then asked: 'After her whom should I serve?' The
Blessed Prophet ﷺ replied: 'Your mother.' He asked this*

same question three times and each time the Blessed Prophet ﷺ gave the same reply. When the man asked the same question a fourth time, the Blessed Prophet ﷺ answered: 'You should serve your father.'

A mother deserves kindness and service even if she is not a Muslim. Asma' bint Abu Bakr ﵂, said: 'My mother who was an idolateress came to me at the time of the treaty with Quraish. I said, "Messenger of Allah! My mother who is ill disposed to Islam has come to me, shall I show her affection?" He replied: "Yes do so."'

The Blessed Prophet ﷺ repeatedly stressed respect for the mother, above all others, because she devotes so much love and self-giving care to her children. Even before they are born she carries them, with great discomfort to herself, and while they are little, she often has to sacrifice her own sleep to comfort and reassure them during the night, and then over many years, till they are old enough to do so themselves, she looks after their many needs. A father naturally commands respect but we must take especial care to show respect to our mother and never displease her. Indeed we should try to be worthy of her prayers for us, because a mother's prayers for her children are accepted by Allah ﷻ.

Elder brother

The Blessed Prophet ﷺ said that an elder brother has the role of a father to his younger brothers and sisters and so should be given similar honour and respect.

Children

People naturally love their children, but if the intention in that love is to obey the commands of Allah ﷻ, then whatever effort parents make, whatever they spend on behalf of their children, will be rewarded. Allah ﷻ has made it a fixed duty for parents to bring up their children in His name and to teach them good things. *The Blessed Prophet ﷺ said: 'Parents should give their children good names and name them after the attributes of Allah ﷻ or after the Prophets. They should bring them up well and help them to marry when they have grown up. If parents fail to do this, they will be answerable to Allah ﷻ. If the children become good Muslims, who observe the Shari'ah, then their prayer for their parents after their death will help them and add to their reward.'*

To bring up a daughter and give her suitable training was especially praised by the Blessed Prophet ﷺ who said: *'Bringing up a daughter acts as a barrier between the parent and the flames of hell. Whoever fosters two daughters nicely will be with me on the Day of Judgement.'* The *Blessed Prophet ﷺ also stated: 'Whoever looks after orphans is just like the one who spends his days and nights in the worship of Allah ﷻ.'*

Another tradition tells that the Blessed Prophet ﷺ said: *'A perfect man of faith is the one who has good morals and is kind to the members of his family.'* He often said: *'The best among you is the one who is good to his family members and I am good to my family.'*

Relatives and elders

Just as it is a duty for a Muslim to respect and serve his parents, so also it is a duty for him to respect and serve his relatives. The Blessed Prophet ﷺ said: *'The highest good is to show respect and serve the friends and companions of your father.'*

Once, a man came to the Blessed Prophet ﷺ and said humbly: 'O Messenger of Allah, I have committed a sin.' The Blessed Prophet ﷺ asked him if his mother was alive. He replied that she was not. Then the Blessed Prophet ﷺ asked the man if his mother's sister (his aunt) was alive. When the man replied that she was alive, the Blessed Prophet ﷺ told him to serve her. This means that to respect and take care of an aunt is similar to serving a mother and leads to the forgiving of sins and to additional blessings.

The Blessed Prophet ﷺ also urged us to remember who our relatives are in order to be able to serve them. This increases mutual love among close family and more distant relatives.

Abu Hurayrah ﷺ reported Allah's Messenger ﷺ as saying: *'Learn enough of your genealogies to show what ties of relationship you should join, for joining ties of relationship is a means of producing love in the family, increasing wealth and prolonging life and he will be remembered well for this even after he has died.'*

Anas ﷺ reported Allah's Messenger ﷺ as saying: *'He who wishes to have his provision enlarged and term of life prolonged, should treat his relatives well.'*

A Muslim should always respect his elders. The Blessed Prophet ﷺ said: *'Anyone who honours old people, Allah ﷻ will honour him in his old age. Anyone who serves old people, people will serve him in his old age.'* And he warned: *'Whoever does not respect his elders and does not show kindness to youngsters is not fit to be called a Muslim.'*

Teachers

It is also our duty to show respect to our teacher who is like our own father. In fact, we should recognize three types of father: our natural father, who is the means of our coming into the world; the 'father' who imparts education to us, our teacher; and the 'father' who gives us his child in marriage, our father-in-law.

Abu Hurayrah ﷺ related that the Prophet ﷺ said: 'Acquire knowledge and for gaining it, learn tranquillity and gravity (seriousness) and be humble and respectful towards the one from whom you are taking the knowledge.' The Prophet ﷺ also said: *'He is not from my community who does not give respect to our elders, does not show mercy to the young and does not show for our knowledgeable their due right of respect and service.'*

Imam Shafi'i said to Sufyan ibn 'Unaynah, may Allah have mercy on both of them, that people come to you from far places to learn and you become angry with them until they leave you. He said: 'They are foolish if they leave that which benefits them to learn because of my bad temper.'

A poet once said: 'A teacher and a physician cannot work wholeheartedly if they are not respected, so if you are not respectful to your physician and your teacher then be patient on your illness and your ignorance.'

Ibn 'Abbas ﷺ *said that because I humbled myself as a student, I was respected when I became a teacher. A student should be careful and mindful of what his teacher is saying even if sometimes he knows the topic which his teacher explains, he should listen as if he doesn't know it. Imam 'Ata' ibn Abi Rabah, may Allah have mercy on him, said: 'Sometimes I listen to a hadith from a person which I may know better than him, still I show as if I don't know. He also said: 'Sometimes a young person relates to me a hadith and I carefully listen to it as if I don't know, while I have heard this hadith even before he was born. There is no difference in the matter of respect towards the teacher whether it is religious knowledge or otherwise because this is the only way to learn and advance in life.*

Neighbours

A Muslim's neighbours have many rights. *The Blessed Prophet* ﷺ *said: 'By Allah, he is not a believer! By Allah, he is not a believer! By Allah, he is not a believer!' He was asked: 'Who is such a man, Messenger of Allah?' He replied: 'The one whose neighbour is not safe from his evil acts.' The Blessed Prophet* ﷺ *also said: 'A man does not deserve to be called a believer if he fills his belly while his neighbour starves.'*

Neighbours are of three kinds: those who have one right, those who have two rights, and those who have three. A

A Muslim relative living in our neighbourhood has three rights: the right of relationship, the right of a neighbour and the right of being a Muslim. A Muslim neighbour who is not a relative has one right as a Muslim and the other as a neighbour. And a non-Muslim neighbour has the right of being a neighbour.

It is the duty of every Muslim to treat all three types of neighbours well. *The Blessed Prophet ﷺ said: 'The messenger of my Lord Jibril عليه السلام continually recommended me to treat neighbours well, till I began to think that neighbours would also be included in the list of inheritors.'* This means that the only difference between a relative and a neighbour is that the relative has a right of inheritance which the neighbour does not. But in respect of good treatment, kindness, affection, help, respect and service, both neighbours and relatives are on an equal footing.

A neighbour does not just mean our next-door neighbour. *The Blessed Prophet ﷺ said that a neighbour-hood extends over forty houses in all directions, though the most deserving is our next-door neighbour.* The right of a neighbour is not limited to just not harming him. It means positively helping and being ready to put oneself out for the neighbour. Just as there is no virtue in bricks and stones which, of themselves, harm no-one, so we can earn virtue only when we actively help our neighbour when he is in need or in trouble.

Imam 'Abdullah ibn Mubarak, may Allah have mercy on him, had a Jewish neighbour who put his house up for sale. When people asked him the price, he said 2000 dinars. They said in astonishment, 'It's only worth 1000 dinars.' The man said, 'You are right, 1000 is the price of the house and 1000 for the neighbourhood of Imam 'Abdullah ibn Mubarak.' When Imam 'Abdullah ibn Mubarak knew that, he called him and gave him the price of the house as a gift and said, 'Please don't sell it.' This is the way our elders lived with their neighbours which is clearly shown in this story.

It is recorded that 'Abdullah ibn 'Amr ﷺ, a devout Companion of the Blessed Prophet ﷺ, one day slaughtered a goat for food. When he was about to sit down for the meal, he enquired if some of the meat had been sent to his Jewish neighbour. When someone asked him why he was making such an enquiry, he said: 'He is my neighbour and the Blessed Prophet ﷺ has stressed that we should treat our neighbour well.' 'Abdullah ibn 'Amr ﷺ would not eat until he was quite sure that some meat had indeed been sent to his neighbour.

Abu Dhar Ghifari ﷺ related that the Blessed Prophet ﷺ said to him: 'Whenever you cook a broth (or soup) add some extra water, then give some to your neighbour.'

The Blessed Prophet ﷺ said: 'Whoever believes in Allah and the Last Day should be good to his neighbour. Whoever believes in Allah and the Last Day should be generous to his guest. Whoever believes in Allah and the Last Day should say what is good or be silent.'

Ibn 'Umar ﷺ said: 'There was a time when no one had a better right to a Muslim's money than his brother Muslim. Nowadays people love their dirhams and dinars more than their brother Muslim. I heard the Blessed Prophet ﷺ

say: "Many a man will be held to account on the Day of Rising by his neighbour calling – 'Lord! This man closed his door to me and denied me human kindness.' " '

Abu Juhayfah ﷺ said: 'A man complained to the Blessed Prophet ﷺ about his neighbour. The Blessed Prophet ﷺ said: 'Take your bags and put them in the road and whoever passes will curse him.' Everyone who passed began to curse that neighbour. Then this man went to the Blessed Prophet ﷺ and told him about the treatment he had met with from the people. The Blessed Prophet ﷺ said: 'Allah's curse is on top of their curse.' Then he said to the one who had complained: 'You have enough' – or something to that effect.

It is a Muslim's duty to respect his neighbour, address him politely, and ask after his welfare, sharing in both his joys and his troubles. If he falls ill we should visit him and call a doctor for him if necessary. If he goes away for a while we should take care of his house and see that his family has enough to eat. We should feel responsible for his children as for our own and take an interest in their education. If he is in need of money we should give him a loan or help him in whatever way we can. If we receive a gift, we should give some of it to him. If he gives something to us we should show that we appreciate it. The Blessed Prophet ﷺ said: 'Do not think a neighbour's gift unimportant, even if he sends a goat's hoof.'

A Muslim should never peep into his neighbour's house or disturb his privacy in any way. He should not try to overhear his private conversations. Because the right attitude is to be thoughtful and considerate, no Muslim should build or extend a house in such a way that it blocks his neighbour's light or air; he should not even fix a nail into his neighbour's wall without his clear permission.

Neighbours see a lot of each other over a long period of time and so get to know each other very well. *That is why the Blessed Prophet ﷺ considered a neighbour to be the best judge of a person's character. He said that if our neighbour praises us then we really are good, but if our neighbour thinks ill of us then we are not.*

Other people in general

We should feel concern for and be prepared to help all Allah's creatures, whether young or old, strong or weak. The misery of any living being should touch us and move us to help, to show care and compassion. It is not proper for a Muslim to see a fellow human being in difficulty and turn away, saying 'It's not my fault; I am not responsible; it's none of my business.' *A Muslim must show mercy; the Blessed Prophet ﷺ commanded it. He said: 'Show mercy to the people of the earth and Allah ﷻ will show mercy to you. One who does not show mercy to the people, Allah ﷻ does not show mercy to him.'*

Followers of every religion claim that they love God, but Allah ﷻ Himself has said that none can excel Muslims in this respect. Therefore, Muslims, as they love Allah ﷻ, must also show love toward their fellow human beings in the field of public service. *The Blessed Prophet ﷺ said: 'Religion teaches that you should be a well-wisher of all. True religion is that you should seek good for everyone.'*

On another occasion he said: *'Whoever does not show mercy to his juniors, does not show respect to his elders, does not speak of good and prevent the spread of evil, is not a good Muslim.'* The Blessed Prophet 🌸 also said: *'The whole nation is like passengers in a boat. If some persons start making holes in the boat, then it is the duty of all others to check them by persuasion or use of force, and take them with themselves; otherwise water will rush in through the holes and all will be drowned.'*

Service to mankind includes providing food for the hungry, sharing other people's burdens, attending to the sick and looking after children, women and the elderly. The Companions of the Blessed Prophet 🌸 were eager to win merit in this way. *A blind woman was heard crying and wailing on the death of the second rightly guided Caliph, Ameer al-Muminin 'Umar Faruq* 🌸. *She said that 'Umar* 🌸 *had been very good to her, that he used to come and fill the water pots, clean the house and put everything in order.* For a great and powerful man to have earned the affection and thanks of a fellow human-being by such simple, ordinary acts of kindness, is a wonderful tribute to his sincerity and humility: for think how much easier it would have been for 'Umar 🌸 not to attend to these things personally but, as the Caliph, get them done by someone else.

A story is told about Mu'tasim-billah, who was the 'Abbasid Caliph. One rainy day he was travelling in the comfort of his carriage when he came upon an old man whose donkey, carrying a heavy load, was stuck in the mud. Mu'tasim got down from his carriage and helped the old man remove the load from the donkey's back and pull the animal from the mud. After he had personally helped in this way he gave the old man a generous gift of money.

Of course, service to others depends on one's ability and one's means in any particular time and place. A doctor can best serve his patients by treating them sympathetically and treating them equally, regardless of whether they are rich or poor, socially weak or powerful. A teacher serves humanity by imparting his knowledge fairly, and with humility, to those who come to him for guidance and instruction. A ruler's duty is to discharge his functions efficiently and honestly. A businessman should take care of the interests of his customers by selling things of good quality, by giving correct measure, and for a moderate profit; he should not cheat his customers, and he should not get into black-marketing or other murky dealings; rather, he should do everything openly and fairly. A farmer, who produces food essential to human life, can best serve his fellow-men by growing good quality produce and getting it quickly to market. To hold back his produce in order to get a better price is both unfair and harmful to others.

A Muslim always has four ways open to him. He can be totally self-serving and uncaring if others are harmed. He can avoid deliberately doing others harm. He can be helpful and kind to others when the chance to do so presents itself. He can deliberately seek out opportunities and situations where he can help others. It is obvious that the Muslim who actively and positively sets out to help others, and not himself, is the most worthy of reward in the next life. It is a high ideal to live up to, but a Muslim must try to live up to it. It does not deepen a person's faith if the best he is prepared to do is to do no harm: a king who never steps out of his palace to find out how others are may well have done no harm, but he has also done no good. That is why a Muslim must meet others, ask after their well-being, and be sympathetic and helpful to the best of his ability. All men and all women are Allah's servants. Whether we are good servants or bad servants is another question.

That question will be asked of us on the Day of Judgement. *An imaginary dialogue between Allah ﷻ and His servants on that Day was narrated by the Blessed Prophet Muhammad ﷺ:*

'Allah ﷻ will say: "O children of Adam! I asked food of you but you did not give it to me." The servants will reply: "O Lord! You are Allah, the Creator, who provides livelihood to all creatures. How can You be in need of food?" Allah ﷻ will say: "That particular man was hungry. He begged you for food but you refused. Had you fed him, that food would have been available to you here."

'Then Allah ﷻ will say: "O sons of Adam! I asked water from you but you did not oblige." The servants will exclaim: "Lord of the worlds! You have created water. You give water to the thirsty. Why do You ask for water?" Allah ﷻ will reply: "A certain servant requested you to give him water but you did not do so. Had you done so, you would have water here."

'Then Allah ﷻ will say: "O children of Adam! I fell ill but you did not visit me." The servants will say: "O All-Mighty Allah! You are the Lord of the Universe. You cure the sick.

How could You fall ill?" Allah ﷻ will reply: "That particular man was sick but you did not look after him. Had you looked after him, you would have found Me with him." '

This teaches us that love for Allah ﷻ demands that, for His sake, we should love and sympathize with His creatures also. We should not go about as if we were deaf and blind to the needs of others. Rather, we should be eager to serve others. *The Blessed Prophet ﷺ said: 'Treat all creatures as the family of Allah ﷻ. Whoever treats His creatures well is loved most by Allah ﷻ.'*

Questions

1. What commands about parents has Allah ﷻ given in the Qur'an?
2. How do parents prepare the way for their children to go to heaven?
3. How should we treat our parents if they have a faith other than Islam?
4. What is the duty of children after the death of their parents?
5. Can you narrate the story of 'Abdullah ibn 'Umar ﷺ?
6. Why did the Blessed Prophet ﷺ reply three times that we should serve our mother?
7. Why is it right and necessary to serve one's mother?
8. What rights do our aunts, uncles and friends of our father enjoy?
9. How should we regard our teacher and our father-in-law?

10. What is the difference between the rights of a neighbour and the rights of a relative?
11. How should we behave with a non-Muslim neighbour?
12. What is the extent of a neighbourhood?
13. What are the responsibilities of a king to his subjects?

-4-

Kindness to Animals

The Blessed Prophet ﷺ was sent as a blessing for all the worlds. He commanded us not only to be kind and merciful to fellow human beings but to all fellow-creatures. *Once he went to a garden and saw a camel so thin its bones were clearly visible through the skin, and its eyes were sunken and hollow. When the camel saw the Blessed Prophet ﷺ it approached him and put its head on his feet. The Blessed Prophet ﷺ was moved by the camel's distress and stroked its head tenderly. Then, he called for the camel's master and said to him: 'Fear Allah ﷻ. Do not torment these speechless creatures. Allah ﷻ has made you their master. It is for you to take care of them and treat them properly. Do not overburden them; work them only as much as they are able. Feed them well and look after them and keep them nicely.'*

The Blessed Prophet ﷺ prohibited unnecessary talk while mounted on a horse or camel. He said: 'Do not make their backs a speaking platform. When you reach your destination, unload them, then say prayers, and after that arrange for their fodder and only then take food yourselves.'

Islam teaches that every living being is under Allah's eye and praises Him. Therefore, we should not tease or abuse any living creature, human or animal. The Blessed Prophet 🕮 narrated a story of a man who, because he had been bitten by an ant, burnt their nest. 'Allah 🕮 said: "You have burnt a community that used to praise Allah 🕮." '

Jabir 🕮 reported that Allah's Messenger 🕮 forbade striking the face and branding on the face.

Ibn 'Umar 🕮 narrated that the Prophet 🕮 cursed those who used a living creature as a target.

'Abdullah bin 'Amr b. Al-'As reported Allah's Messenger 🕮 as saying that if you kill a sparrow or anything greater, wrong-fully, Allah will question you about killing it. On being asked what was the right way he replied: 'He should eat it.'

Shaddad b. Aus reported Allah's Messenger 🕮 as saying, 'Allah the Blessed and Exalted has decreed that every-thing should be done in a good way, so when you kill use a good method for each of you should sharpen his knife and give the animal as little pain as possible.'

Ibn 'Umar 🕮 told how he heard Allah's Messenger 🕮 prohibit keeping an animal or anything else waiting to be killed. There are many traditions that teach us about being kind to animals. Here are some:

The Blessed Prophet 🕮 said: 'There was a woman of loose character. One day she came across a dog who was dying of thirst. She felt great pity for the dog but could not find any water to quench its thirst. At last she was able to find a well but there was neither rope nor bucket to draw water. She was at a loss what to do. Then she remembered *that she was wearing leather socks. She took off one sock and tied it to the end of her scarf, and threw it down the well. In this way she was able to draw water from the well. Then she gently and slowly poured the water into the dog's mouth. The dog regained its strength, stood up and put its head on the woman's feet. Allah ﷻ then blessed the woman in such a way that she gave up all her bad habits, asked for forgiveness from Allah ﷻ and became a virtuous woman. Allah ﷻ then pardoned all her sins.' Then, the Blessed Prophet ﷺ added: 'I have seen her in paradise.'*

Allah's Messenger ﷺ, also narrated this story, about a pious woman. But this woman had an unfeeling heart. She kept a cat in her house to keep away the rats. But she did not give the cat anything to eat and it often ran away to look for food. To stop it running away, the woman tied the cat with a rope but still did not feed it. The poor cat, with nothing to eat, survived for only a few days and finally died of hunger. The Blessed Prophet ﷺ commented: 'I have seen this woman in hell.'

Another story tells about Nasiruddin who was the slave of a king, and very fond of hunting. One day he came across a very pretty baby deer and picked it up and rode away. The mother deer saw Nasiruddin take her baby and followed him anxiously. Nasiruddin, pleased with the baby deer, was thinking about presenting it to his children to play with. After a time, he chanced to look back and saw the mother deer following him, her expression full of grief. He noticed too that she did not seem to care about her own safety. Moved to pity, Nasiruddin set the baby deer free. The mother deer nuzzled and licked her baby fondly and the two deer together leapt happily away into the forest. But many times the mother deer looked back at Nasiruddin, as if to express her thanks.

That night Nasiruddin dreamt that the revered Prophet ﷺ, was addressing him: 'Nasiruddin, your name has been entered in the list of Allah ﷻ, and you will one day have a kingdom. But remember that when you are a king you will also have many responsibilities. Just as you have shown mercy to the deer today, you should be merciful to all Allah's creatures. You should not forget your people by falling into a life of luxury.'

This dream came true and Nasiruddin did become king, Amir Nasiruddin Subaktagin, father of the famous Sultan Mahmud the Gazanavid who conquered India for Islam and ruled it with justice and integrity. The moral of the story is that if we wish Allah ﷻ to be merciful to us, we must be eager to show mercy to all the living creatures of the earth.

Questions

1. What are the responsibilities of human beings towards animals?
2. Why was a sinful woman granted forgiveness?
3. How did she draw water from the well?
4. Can you narrate the story of Nasiruddin and the baby deer?
5. Can you narrate a story of your own about kindness to animals?

– 5 –

Rights and Duties

People have rights on each other and duties to each other. If we share a house with our parents, brothers, sisters and elders, then there are certain duties which have to be performed by them for us, and certain duties which we have to discharge for them. These are known as mutual rights and duties. Beyond the house, our neighbours and countrymen also have mutual rights and duties.

Since Allah ﷻ has created all things, including ourselves, and all the means for our survival and well-being, He has primary rights on us. The Blessed Prophet Muhammad ﷺ has taught us many things for our well-being in this life and in the life to come. Therefore, we have duties to him. Similarly, our parents, who have brought us up with much hard work, love and care, also have rights on us. Our teachers also have rights on us because they show us the light of knowledge and open up new avenues for our development. Brothers, sisters, relatives and neighbours who assist our parents and help us whenever they can also have rights on us. Similarly, we owe a duty to the people of our locality who help us, for without them our lives would become isolated and dull, and without their help to keep law and order, we would be at the mercy of thieves and robbers. In fact all the services that we all need and use, things like, for example, schools, hospitals, post offices, roads, railways, communications, street lighting, the police, the army, are provided by ourselves and our fellow citizens acting together. Thus in social life we all help each other and are tied or 'obligated' to each other.

Every Muslim must acknowledge these rights and discharge his duties. *The Blessed Prophet ﷺ said: 'Discharge your duties to those whom you owe.'*

How to discharge our duties

We have spoken of the countless blessings Allah ﷻ has given us. He has also asked us to perform certain duties. If we are able to discharge them well, He generously accepts our efforts as our humble acknowledgement.

The most appropriate and desirable way of discharging our duty of thanks to Allah ﷻ is to worship Him alone and not associate anyone with Him. We should prostrate ourselves before only Him. Our fasting, our alms-giving, our pilgrimage should be exclusively for Him.

Next to Allah ﷻ, we are indebted to the Blessed Prophet Muhammad ﷺ, Allah's Messenger on earth. Allah ﷻ has commanded that we should follow the example of the Blessed Prophet ﷺ in all that we do. We should behave as he has taught us on occasions of happiness, or grief, at festivals and on every day of our life. However hard it sometimes seems, we should love and respect him more than we do our parents, children, relatives, friends and being or becoming rich. In fact, it is only if we do that, that we can consistently abide by his example. Also, it is our duty to pray to Allah ﷻ to send His blessings on the Blessed Prophet Muhammad ﷺ and his descendants and sincere followers. When we say that prayer we are, in fact, stating our respect for the whole way of life that the Blessed Prophet ﷺ set up, and our agreement to live by it.

In a way our most important duty as Muslims is to do nothing that might bring disrespect to Islam, to the Blessed Prophet ﷺ and to our family. Rather, we should do our best to bring credit to our family and to the way of life of Islam. It is important then for a Muslim to remember that he is not free to do as he pleases, being responsible to no-one but himself. Quite the opposite: he is tied, obliged, answerable. Keeping that in mind means going about responsibly, carefully, constantly aware of one's debt to Allah ﷻ, to the Blessed Prophet ﷺ, to one's fellow-Muslims, to all the people who do so much for us. The first and foremost duty that debt imposes on us is the duty of gratitude or giving thanks.

Gratitude

To show gratitude to Allah ﷻ means to recognize all His blessings. Eyes, nose, ears, tongue, hands, feet, teeth, fingers and every other part of our bodies are all blessings from Him. Their value is realized when any of them is lost or impaired. How long and energetically we try to cure the diseases which affect our bodies! Who would exchange one of his eyes for a mountain of gold or silver? Therefore it is the duty of every human being to recognize each blessing and thank Allah ﷻ who gave it. Likewise, the clothes we wear, the place where we sleep, wherever we find shelter from the sun or rain, or where we wash or bath, or where we pray, the food we eat, are all blessings for which we should acknowledge our debt to Allah ﷻ.

But it is not only material things that we should be grateful for. If something happens to hurt our feelings, we go to our parents, or brother or sister, or relative, friend or neighbour, and we do so looking for and expecting their sympathy. They console us, embrace us and draw us near to them. We are warmed and restored by this love and affection which, also worth more than gold and silver, is part of our debt to Allah ﷻ.

Allah ﷻ needs no repayment. Every joint of every limb, every beat of the heart, every breath, is a favour from Allah ﷻ. His blessings are too many to count, let alone repay. We can at best show our gratitude to Allah ﷻ. To do that, we must devote ourselves body and mind, and belongings, to observing His commands. We must recite His name and remember Him in our hearts. And we can show our thanks also by using the talents and time Allah ﷻ has given us to benefit our fellow-creatures, for these talents and this time are not only privileges but also responsibilities.

Good health is a great blessing. Its duty on us is to do a good day's work, to attend to the sick, to share our neighbours' burdens and generally be helpful and cheerful. Wealth is also a valuable blessing. Its obligation is that we should help the needy, pay alms, give loans without interest and spend freely on social welfare. But we should never boast of our generosity because, in Allah's eyes, we have simply done our duty, transferred from ourselves to others what in reality belongs wholly to Allah ﷻ: for we are only the caretakers of our property, not outright owners.

Being able to read and write or literacy is another blessing which we can acknowledge by helping to make others literate. If an illiterate person comes to us, we should write or read for him and thank Allah ﷻ that we are more able than him in this matter, and that we have been of some use to others.

A ruler or anyone in a position of authority should always deal justly, have mercy on those under him, overlook their faults and omissions, strive to lighten their burdens, and positively work for their well-being. Above all, a person in authority must not be haughty towards those he or she has authority over.

Once a Companion asked the Blessed Prophet ﷺ: 'O Messenger of Allah ﷺ! If my servant commits any wrong, how many times should I pardon him?' The Blessed Prophet ﷺ replied: 'Seventy times each day.' That is something we should remember when we wish Allah ﷻ to pardon our sins seventy times a day.

It is wrong to forget the one who has given us blessings and instead praise others. For example, our parents have brought us up, and it is our duty to show thanks to them. But if, instead, we start heaping thanks and praises on their enemies, we would not only be acting foolishly but also doing a most serious wrong. How much more serious a wrong is it to forget Allah ﷻ and worship some false god or goddess instead. This is called an unforgivable sin in the Qur'an. And how could it be forgiven, seeing that the person who does not pray wholly to Allah ﷻ cannot pray to Him for forgiveness either?

For example, if a couple are blessed with a child, on the seventh day of his birth they should express their thanks to Allah ﷻ by sacrificing a goat in the name of Allah ﷻ for His blessing and shaving the child's head (*aqiqah*) and distributing food and gifts among the needy of their neighbourhood and, in that generous way, share their happiness with the poor, the orphans and widows. But if, instead, the couple celebrate the occasion by allowing the sort of music and dancing or other activities prohibited by the law of Islam, it means they are in reality praising Allah's enemy, and going against Allah ﷻ.

Another form of going against Allah ﷻ is to waste the resources He has given us, because Allah ﷻ has expressly and most strictly condemned those who waste the time and resources He has lent to them in order to test them: such wasters are referred to in the Qur'an as 'brothers of the devil':

وَءَاتِ ذَا ٱلْقُرْبَىٰ حَقَّهُۥ وَٱلْمِسْكِينَ وَٱبْنَ ٱلسَّبِيلِ وَلَا تُبَذِّرْ تَبْذِيرًا ﴿٢٦﴾ إِنَّ ٱلْمُبَذِّرِينَ كَانُوٓاْ إِخْوَٰنَ ٱلشَّيَٰطِينِ وَكَانَ ٱلشَّيْطَٰنُ لِرَبِّهِۦ كَفُورًا ﴿٢٧﴾

Give your relatives their due (what you owe to them), and to the needy, and to those travelling, and do not be wantonly wasteful. Listen! Those who waste (what Allah ﷻ has given them) have always been the devil's brothers, and the devil has always been a thankless being, ungrateful to his Lord. [Bani Isra'il 17: 26-7]

If somebody we have done a favour for respects us and tries to please us, we feel happy. We would be pleased to do him more favours if the opportunity arose. But if he, instead of acknowledging our kindness, disobeys us and displeases us by doing what we do not like, it is obvious that instead of helping him again we might even prefer not to have done him the favour.

Thankfulness leads to greater humanity in one's dealings with others, as well as reward in the life to come. Being thankless leads to meanness and misfortune in human relations, and in the life to come is severely punished:

$$وَإِذْ تَأَذَّنَ رَبُّكُمْ لَئِن شَكَرْتُمْ لَأَزِيدَنَّكُمْ ۖ وَلَئِن كَفَرْتُمْ إِنَّ عَذَابِى لَشَدِيدٌ ۝$$

And when your Lord proclaimed: If you are thankful, surely I will increase you, but if you are thankless My chastisement is surely terrible. [Ibrahim 14: 7]

The Blessed Prophet ﷺ spent his days in prayer, teaching, preaching, and in the service of others. At night, instead of resting, he prayed to Allah ﷻ, standing for long hours with the result that his feet would become swollen.

Once, 'A'ishah Siddiqah ﷺ asked him: 'O Messenger of Allah ﷺ! You are infallible and free from sin. Allah ﷻ has expressly stated in the Qur'an that He has forgiven all your mistakes. Why then do you say such long prayers and endure so much pain?' The Blessed Prophet ﷺ replied: 'O 'A'ishah, should I not become a grateful servant?' The Blessed Prophet's reply meant that a true servant of Allah ﷻ should express his thankfulness for the many divine blessings he receives, because doing so is a vital part of being a sincere servant of Allah ﷻ.

The Blessed Prophet ﷺ thanked Allah ﷻ after every occasion of prayer. But he also explained how important it is for a Muslim to be thankful to his fellow human- beings: 'One who does not acknowledge the favour of human beings cannot be grateful to Allah ﷻ.' This is a simple truth. The kindness and favours of relatives and friends are obvious to us. But while the blessings and favours of Allah ﷻ are manifold, no-one is able to see Him giving these rewards. It needs understanding to realize and acknowledge them as favours from Him. Therefore we should practise the habit of being grateful so that we may thank Allah ﷻ and become sincere servants.

Questions

1. What are mutual rights and duties?
2. Who has primary rights on us and why?
3. What is our most important duty as Muslims?
4. Can you define indebtedness or gratitude?
5. Why are certain people described in the Qur'an as 'brothers of the devil'?
6. What is the proper way of acknowledging favour or kindness?
7. Why is it that someone who does not show thanks to his fellow human-beings, cannot be thankful to Allah ﷻ?

- 6 -

Truth and Falsehood

The Messenger of Allah 🕌, said: 'A Muslim must not be a liar.' And he explained why: 'Truth leads a man to the path of virtue, which leads him to paradise. Falsehood pulls a man to sin and sin throws him into hell.'

It is very important then for a Muslim to be careful what he says, when and to whom. He must weigh his words and make sure that what he says is true. The tongue may be only a small part of our body but its use has the most serious consequences. If we abuse someone or show anger, the other person may abuse us back or even start a fight. Many a careless remark about a group has led to clashes and resulted in bloodshed.

The Blessed Prophet 🕌 said that every morning each limb of the body requests the tongue to behave well, as its good behaviour keeps the body safe and secure, while its mis-behaviour can cause the body harm. He also said: 'To check one's tongue is a great act of piety.' Once, the Blessed Prophet 🕌 related many good things to one of his Companions, Mu'adh ⚘. Then he took hold of his tongue and said: 'Mu'adh, be afraid of it.' Mu'adh ⚘ said: 'O Messenger of Allah! Why should we fear the tongue?' The

Blessed Prophet ﷺ *replied: 'Because a man is liable to be condemned to hell because of its misdeeds and slips.'*

Keeping promises

A Muslim should be very cautious about what promises he makes, because if he makes a promise, he must keep it, even if it proves difficult to do so. The Blessed Prophet Muhammad ﷺ always spoke the truth and kept his word, and because of that was widely respected and given the title 'the trustworthy'. He said: *'One who does not keep his word is not a man of faith.'* In the Qur'an too, Allah ﷻ has stressed many times that believers must keep their word.

Once, the Blessed Prophet ﷺ *and another man were discussing a matter when the man was called away, so he asked the Blessed Prophet* ﷺ *to wait a short while until he returned. However, the man became so absorbed in his work that it was much later that he remembered that he had asked the Blessed Prophet* ﷺ *to wait for him. When he reached the place he found the Blessed Prophet* ﷺ *still there. Because of his lapse, the man expected the Blessed Prophet* ﷺ *to be angry and rebuke him, but the Blessed Prophet* ﷺ *said softly to him: 'Brother, where were you? I have been waiting here for a long time.'*

The greatest promise a Muslim makes is to be true to Islam, to carry out the commands of Allah ﷻ and follow the *Sunnah*, the example of the Blessed Prophet ﷺ. Obviously, if in a rash moment, someone makes a promise to do something that is against the law of Islam, then that promise must not be kept. Suppose, in a moment of unthinking anger, a Muslim threatened to beat up someone or to never speak to him again, or something similar. In this case, the Muslim should apologize and make up for it, *both* for the unlawful promise and for breaking it.

Malik ﷺ, a Companion of the Blessed Prophet ﷺ, once came to him and asked: 'O Messenger of Allah! One day I went to get help from a cousin of mine but he flatly refused. This annoyed me so much I swore never to help him. But now he has come to me to seek my help. What should I do?' The Blessed Prophet ﷺ advised him: 'You should do whatever is better. Help your cousin and pay the penalty for breaking your vow.'

False oaths

Sometimes a Muslim will swear by the name of Allah ﷻ, the Qur'an and the faith, to show that he is speaking the truth. But to swear an oath in this way is not wise. If we tell a lie, then by using Allah's name we are both cheating the people and disgracing Allah's name. However, if on some special occasion we are asked to swear to the truth of a thing then we can do so. *The Blessed Prophet ﷺ said: 'To take false oath is a major sin, like associating someone with Allah ﷻ.'*

Only swearing by the name of Allah ﷻ is allowed. All other forms, such as swearing by our faith, by the Qur'an, by Makkah, by any person such as a father or mother, or by any other religion, are improper. If the occasion demands that we must take an oath, then it must be only in Allah's name.

A truthful youth

A young man, named 'Abdul-Qadir, wanted very much to get a good religious education. As there was no teacher or institution in his city where he could get knowledge, and his father had died, it was to his mother that he had to go for permission to leave. He asked to go to Baghdad, which at that time was a big metropolitan city, with many world-famous libraries and educational institutions, and many renowned scholars and divines lived there. 'Abdul-Qadir pleaded with his mother. He argued that an uneducated person cannot command respect, that, in certain ways, an illiterate is ignorant of both religious and worldly affairs. He said that ignorance is a sort of death, for it is empty of light. Knowledge, he said, is true light, without which one cannot even pray properly, that is, with full understanding.

His mother was a very virtuous lady, devoted to reciting the Qur'an and the names of Allah ﷻ. She was pleased that 'Abdul-Qadir had such a strong desire for learning and readily agreed that he should go to Baghdad. She arranged provisions for the journey and sewed forty gold coins, all the money she had, in the inner lining of his coat-sleeve so that they could not be easily detected. When he was ready to leave, she committed him to the care of Allah ﷻ and offered him some advice: she told him to always be truthful, to live by the truth always, and to never forget this advice.

In those days people travelled on camel, horse-back or on foot. For protection against thieves and robbers, travellers often journeyed together in a caravan. A caravan was about to set out for Baghdad and 'Abdul-Qadir joined it. But on the journey the caravan was attacked by robbers. One robber took 'Abdul-Qadir's luggage, then demanded: 'What else do you have?' 'Abdul-Qadir replied very calmly: 'I have forty gold coins.' The robber asked if he was joking. 'Abdul-Qadir denied that he was joking for he remembered the advice of his mother to always speak the truth. He reminded himself that he was going on a noble mission to get an education, which is an act of piety leading to paradise; that angels have great respect for students and for scholars who are the successors of the Prophets, and that he was going to be one of them. So he had decided to risk everything, his life if necessary, but to tell the truth about the forty gold coins.

Meanwhile another robber came up and, shaking 'Abdul-Qadir roughly, said: 'What money do you have?' 'Abdul-Qadir replied, as before, that he had forty gold coins. He spoke so calmly that the robber was quite taken aback. He too thought at first that he was joking, but he soon realized that one so young would not behave in quite this way when his very life could be in danger. Puzzled, the robber thought it wiser to pass the matter on to his chief.

The robber-chief was also taken aback when he heard about 'Abdul-Qadir's strange behaviour. He took a long look at him. He appeared to be a calm, straightforward young man with common sense and signs of a good nature. Speaking politely, the robber-chief asked the youth's name and why he was travelling with the caravan. The youth answered: 'My name is 'Abdul-Qadir, I come from Jilan and I am going to Baghdad to get an education.'

Then the robber-chief asked him if he had any money with him. 'Abdul-Qadir told him that he had forty gold coins, concealed in the sleeve of his coat. The chief was surprised and asked him why he had told him about the coins. 'Abdul-Qadir replied that being a Muslim he could not tell a lie.

His reply struck at the heart of the robber-chief who suddenly felt ashamed and began to awaken from his ignorance. He said to himself: How earnestly and faithfully this young lad follows the commands of Islam, while I, a fully grown man, though I have a Muslim name, bring disgrace to Islam! He is not prepared to tell a single lie while we lead a life of continual lying and sin. We torment Allah's creatures and rob them of their hard-earned wealth.

Shame on such a way of life! Tears welled in his eyes and he hung his head in shame. Then, looking up, he asked forgiveness of 'Abdul-Qadir. Now it was 'Abdul-Qadir's turn to be overwhelmed. In a voice full of feeling he said: 'Why do you ask forgiveness of me? You must pray to Allah ﷻ and show Him that you feel badly about your crimes against His creatures, and mean never to do them again.'

After that, the robber-chief took a vow before 'Abdul-Qadir to lead a virtuous life. His fellow-robbers also asked pardon of the other members of the caravan and restored all their belongings. In this way, they became good, law-abiding Muslims.

If 'Abdul-Qadir had not spoken the truth, he would not have displayed the calm and strength that so surprised the robbers. If he had tried to hide behind a lie, he would have been nervous, the robbers would certainly have become suspicious and then, after searching 'Abdul- Qadir they would have, if they found the gold coins, at least severely punished, perhaps even killed, him. By telling the truth, 'Abdul-Qadir saved his honour as well as his money. More important, because of the way he told the truth, because of his firmness and sincerity, he was able to touch the hearts of the robbers. They repented as a result, returned what they had stolen from the other travellers, and started to reform themselves.

The story shows very well how sticking to the truth can lead Muslims on the way to paradise in the life to come. And the wise youth in the story became one of the most saintly and most respected men in Muslim history: he is remembered as Shaikh 'Abdul-Qadir Jilani, may Allah have mercy on him.

Questions

1. What can telling the truth lead to? And telling lies?
2. What did the Blessed Prophet ﷺ say about keeping one's word?
3. What do our limbs say to our tongue every morning, and why?
4. What advice did the Blessed Prophet ﷺ give to Mu'adh ؟
5. What must a Muslim do if he is unable to keep a solemn promise?
6. What is the supreme promise a Muslim makes and must always keep?

7. Why is it wrong to fulfil a promise to do an un-lawful act?
8. How serious a sin is swearing a false oath?
9. What is the only form of oath permitted in Islam?
10. Can you name the virtues of knowledge?
11. What advice did 'Abdul-Qadir's mother give him?
12. Why did 'Abdul-Qadir decide not to tell a lie when he was questioned by the robbers?
13. What might have happened if 'Abdul-Qadir had lied?

- 7 -

Habits, Good and Bad

A person's habits are like the air he breathes, simply there, a part of the background; they are actions he does without the conscious decision to do them, and which he will think are acceptable for no other reason than that he is used to them. In the same way, people get used to foul air because they have been breathing it so long they can no longer remember what clean air was like. If many others share the same habits, they seem more than acceptable, they seem *right*. And that is the danger of habits, they establish patterns of what is right and wrong, without anybody having really thought about them.

For a Muslim it is of the greatest importance that he derives his actions from the commands of the Qur'an and the example of the Blessed Prophet ﷺ.

It is not good just to do things because other people around you do them; similarly, it is not good to ignore things because other people around you do not do them.

As we said in the first chapter, for a Muslim the test of an action is not popular custom, the test is to judge that action against the commands of the Qur'an and the

Sunnah of the Blessed Prophet ﷺ. This is even more important in the case of habits, the actions you do day after day.

Choosing the right company

Because, at least partly, your actions and your habits depend on the company you keep, it is vital for a Muslim to choose the right company. Free-mixing between boys and girls is not allowed. *The Blessed Prophet ﷺ said: 'A person follows his friend.'*

What this means is that a person naturally takes after the company he keeps. If you keep bad company, if you spend your time with those who neglect their prayers, who waste their time, who do things unlawful in Islam, the very best that can happen is that you will become easy-going about things, start to think them normal, and then it will be that much harder for you to do the right things. And the worst that can happen is that you will yourself start to neglect your prayers, to waste time, to do things unlawful in Islam, and eventually these things will become habitual.

The Blessed Prophet ﷺ said: 'A good companion is like a perfume seller.' Spending your day in good company is like spending your day in a perfume shop: you will at the end of the day smell, perhaps faintly, perhaps strongly, of perfume.

In the same way, spending your day in bad company is like spending the day at the side of a person who works the bellows. The bellows may burn your clothing, or you may get a bad smell. Because that is bound to happen, it is wiser, if only for the sake of your good name, to avoid bad company. The Blessed Prophet ﷺ said: 'Don't go near a place that has a doubtful reputation (and so risk yourself) being accused.'

Good habits: personal dignity and cleanliness

There are examples in many places in this book of the habits of mind or attitudes which it is proper for a Muslim to encourage in himself and in others. The basic principle behind most of these attitudes is to regard others as more important than oneself, to be modest, moderate, humble, to be strict with oneself, forgiving with others.

In everyday actions, the basic principle behind good habits recommended to Muslims is *composure*, a sense of one's dignity as a Muslim. Being composed means being deliberate in one's actions, steady, unhurried. People who rush through their prayers because they have a lazy attitude to saying them, are criticized in the Qur'an. It is better to arrive at the mosque a little late, but calm and collected, than to arrive just on time but red-faced and flustered from running. It is best, of course, to be there early, which requires organizing your affairs properly for that purpose. Indeed, it is partly to teach composure that the five daily prayers were instituted in Islam.

What most naturally expresses a person's sense of his own dignity is how he lets himself be seen by others. For this reason, there are rules that a Muslim must observe about dress and personal hygiene or cleanliness. Also, to show how important these matters are, they are linked with *salah* or the five daily prayers. The link is *wudu*. It is not necessary here to give the details of *wudu* and dress, as most readers will be familiar with them. But it is obvious that if a Muslim remembers that he has soon to pray, he will keep himself and his clothes clean; for the same reason, he will keep the place where he lives clean, and avoid, so far as he can, doing things or going to places after which he will be dirty and therefore unable to pray. From the regular practice of *wudu* and *salah*, a Muslim learns not 'to let himself go', to look or be sloppy or dirty, but to be deliberately orderly in whatever he is doing.

Cleanliness is a necessary part of hygiene, that is, of being clean in order to be healthy. Because human beings live in groups, large or small, cleanliness becomes an act of consideration, of caring, for others' health and comfort as well as one's own.

A Muslim should always, for example, carry a handkerchief so that he can protect others from any infection he may be carrying, by using that handkerchief when he coughs or sneezes. It is a *Sunnah* to praise Allah ﷻ after sneezing, say: *alhamdulillah*, because of the relief it brings. Out of consideration for others also, a Muslim should ensure that neither his body nor his breath give off smells that could be offensive: regular cleaning of teeth is recommended for this reason, likewise avoiding those habits (for example, eating raw onions or garlic, smoking) which cause bad breath. Because disease is carried in human hair, a Muslim is recommended not to let it grow too long and to wash and groom it regularly. Certain (usually nervous) habits, like biting fingernails, tittering, giggling, and also whistling at people, often make others uneasy and should be avoided.

The desire to be independent, to fend for oneself, goes with having a sense of one's dignity as a Muslim. In fact, people naturally prefer to do things for themselves, they take pleasure in it, but in certain social classes and in certain moods people allow themselves to become sloppy and prefer, instead, to watch others work, and to do nothing for themselves.

The Blessed Prophet Muhammad ﷺ, though busy with the weightiest public affairs, still made time to mend his own cloak, to repair his own shoes, to milk the goats, to help in the house, and so on. Far from being beneath a Muslim's dignity to do these things, they are a measure of it: that is why the Blessed Prophet ﷺ set the example himself.

His beloved daughter, Fatimah ﷺ, a most virtuous and gentle lady of whom the Blessed Prophet ﷺ said, she would be the leader of all the women in Paradise, did all her housework herself, she herself carried waterskins on her shoulders, and herself ground flour to make bread.

Two dangerous habits:

(i) back-biting

The Blessed Prophet ﷺ was asked to explain what back-biting is. He said: 'Back-biting means to speak of your brother (fellow-Muslim) in his absence in such a way that it hurts his feelings.' One of the Companions asked: 'O Messenger of Allah! if a person really has the quality (for example, if a man is called a habitual liar in his absence and he is a habitual liar), then what is the position?' The Blessed Prophet ﷺ replied: 'This is called back-biting. If the person does not have that habit, then it will be a false accusation.'

Thus, to say something about a person in his absence that would, if he heard it, hurt his feelings, to call him stupid, to point out some bodily defects or defects in his character or dress or family history or in his house, or any other such thing whether true or not, is back-biting. If a Muslim suggests that a person has certain faults when in fact he has not, then that Muslim commits two sins: one of false accusation, and the other of back-biting.

Back-biting is not confined only to words. For example, if someone does not actually call another blind or one-eyed but hints at it by gesture, this also constitutes back-biting and is prohibited. *Once, 'A'ishah ﷺ, the wife of the Blessed Prophet ﷺ, was talking about a woman who was short in height: she did not say that the woman was short but indicated as much by a scornful gesture. The Blessed Prophet ﷺ immediately criticized her: 'What you have done, if it were thrown into the sea, would make it filthy.'*

Back-biting is so severely criticized because it is a source of evil for the community. It leads to mistrust between people. Once a person gets a reputation for back-biting, others will avoid him because they realize that he will probably also talk about them behind their backs. Also, if you hear something bad about a person, even someone you do not know, it may, however hard you try, make you prejudiced against that person. This is obviously bad because it prevents people from making true judgements and from approaching each other trustingly.

Back-biting is criticized also because it not only causes injustice, it is itself an act of injustice. A person who back-bites often does so to focus attention from his own faults. Only Allah ﷻ is free of all faults and shortcomings. A Muslim must keep this always in mind and look to his own failings rather than others'.

A third reason why back-biting is an evil is that it is a cowardly act. People back-bite because they are not brave enough to face the person they are criticizing with their criticism. They make the faults of others a way of passing the time, a subject of idle conversation, a form of entertainment, instead of trying to help the person who has the fault, if he really has it, to put it right. A good Muslim who means well should take his fellow-Muslim to one side, where no-one else can hear, and explain what is wrong. In this way, that person will feel that the criticism is being made out of genuine concern for him, to make him better or to put right his fault, and not to make him look bad or foolish in the eyes of others.

Malik bin Dinar ؓ was a famous Imam. Once, a dog came and sat near him. Someone wanted to chase the dog away, but he said: 'Leave it. It is better than a friend who back-bites.' In the Qur'an back-biting is compared to eating the dead flesh of a fellow-Muslim:

يَـٰٓأَيُّهَا ٱلَّذِينَ ءَامَنُوا ٱجْتَنِبُوا كَثِيرًا مِّنَ ٱلظَّنِّ إِنَّ بَعْضَ ٱلظَّنِّ إِثْمٌ ۖ وَلَا تَجَسَّسُوا وَلَا يَغْتَب بَّعْضُكُم بَعْضًا ۚ أَيُحِبُّ أَحَدُكُمْ أَن يَأْكُلَ لَحْمَ أَخِيهِ مَيْتًا فَكَرِهْتُمُوهُ ۚ وَٱتَّقُوا ٱللَّهَ ۚ إِنَّ ٱللَّهَ تَوَّابٌ رَّحِيمٌ ﴿١٢﴾

O believers! Stay clear of suspicion as much (as possible): for, in some cases, suspicion is a sin. And do not spy on each other, or say harmful things about each other, behind your backs. Would any of you like to eat the flesh of his dead brother? No, you would be sick at the thought of it. But fear Allah: for Allah is oft-Returning, Most Merciful.
[al-Hujurat 49: 12]

When the Blessed Prophet ﷺ *ascended through the heavens (Mi'raj), he saw some people scrubbing their faces and chests with copper nails. The Angel Jibril* عليه السلام *told him that these were persons who slandered others and talked ill of them in their absence.*

The Blessed Prophet ﷺ *also stated that back-biting destroys a man's other virtues just like fire consumes dry grass.* It seems a minor sin but it has the gravest consequences. That is why a Muslim is prohibited from back-biting against another person, Muslim or non-Muslim.

(ii) Spreading false rumours

Similar to back-biting, carrying tales or spreading rumours is a very grave sin, dangerous to the community because, by inciting people against each other it can destroy families and even countries. *The Blessed Prophet* ﷺ *said that a person who carries tales will not be permitted to enter heaven.*

Just because of a false rumour, the great city of Delhi in India suffered a terrible massacre. The Mogul king who ruled Delhi, called Muhammad Shah Rangeela, used to spend all his time in his own pleasures, did not care about the people's welfare, and let his country slide into ruin.

The king of Iran, Nadir Shah, came to know of this and, sensing an easy victory, invaded India.

Shah Rangeela's forces were defeated and Nadir Shah soon captured Delhi. However, he did not replace Muhammad Shah as king but instead entered into a treaty of friendship. To celebrate the treaty a feast was held in the Red Fort, and was attended by both kings, their ministers and officials. Later that night, someone started a rumour that Nadir Shah had been killed. The people of Delhi believed the rumour and, seeing a chance for revenge, started killing Nadir Shah's soldiers. When Nadir Shah heard of the fighting he rushed to the scene, but by then even his appearance failed to stop the people of Delhi from attacking his soldiers. He could not tolerate the continuing attack on his men and ordered his soldiers to kill the citizens of Delhi. In the massacre that followed the streets of Delhi flowed with blood. Thousands of innocent people were slaughtered.

This terrible event came about because someone told a lie about the death of Nadir Shah and because people accepted the rumour without checking if it was true. The Qur'an has strictly prohibited spreading a rumour without first confirming that it is correct. Any such news should first be told to a wise and experienced person, and only after that person has carefully checked and confirmed it, should it be passed to others or made public:

يَـٰٓأَيُّهَا ٱلَّذِينَ ءَامَنُوٓا۟ إِن جَآءَكُمْ فَاسِقٌۢ بِنَبَإٍ فَتَبَيَّنُوٓا۟ أَن تُصِيبُوا۟ قَوْمًۢا بِجَهَـٰلَةٍ فَتُصْبِحُوا۟ عَلَىٰ مَا فَعَلْتُمْ نَـٰدِمِينَ ﴿٦﴾

O believers! If an ill-meaning person comes to you with some news, make sure of the truth (of it), in case you harm people without knowing it, and afterwards become full of remorse for what you have done. [al-Hujurat 49: 6]

The Blessed Prophet ﷺ *said: 'It is a lie to start spreading whatever you hear.' It is not permitted to lie even in fun. The Blessed Prophet* ﷺ *warned: 'Whoever spreads false news to make others laugh is liable to destruction.'* Similarly, deceit is also prohibited. *The Blessed Prophet* ﷺ *said: 'The worst deceit is to lie to a friend who trusts in you and believes you to be speaking the truth.'*

It is easy to appreciate how important a duty it is for every Muslim to positively follow the truth. He should seek out the truth and then act on it; and when he speaks make sure he is speaking the truth. *The Blessed Prophet* ﷺ *said: 'Such a person would be called ever-truthful by Allah* ﷻ. *May Allah* ﷻ *make us follow the path of truth.'*

Questions

1. Why is it necessary for a Muslim to deliberately model his habits according to the commands of the Qur'an and the example of the Blessed Prophet ﷺ?
2. What happens if a Muslim does not do this? Where does he get his habits from?
3. What are the effects of having good companions?
4. What are the dangers of bad company?
5. In what ways can a Muslim express dignity through his dress and personal habits?
6. What are the benefits in a Muslim's everyday life of *wudu* and *salah*?
7. What is meant by back-biting?
8. What did the Blessed Prophet ﷺ witness on his ascent through the heavens (*Mi'raj*)?
9. Why is back-biting such a grave sin?
10. What was the result of the rumour spread in Delhi about Nadir Shah?
11. How should a rumour be treated to assess its correctness?

-8-

Courtesies

Greeting others

If we keep in mind that the reason for greeting others is to make and maintain friendly relationships between Muslims, and between Muslims and non-Muslims, it is easy to understand why Muslim greetings are as they are. Humility about oneself and consideration for the other person is the first principle.

Thus, a Muslim should speak in a mild, self-controlled but clear voice, and his manner should express warmth and sincerity. The words to use are: *as-salamu 'alaykum wa rahmatullahi wa barakatuh*, which mean 'peace be upon you and Allah's mercy and His blessings'. It is the fairest of all greetings in the world and, spoken from the heart, is a virtuous act that is rewarded both in this life (in friendship and mutual respect between persons) and in the life to come.

The Blessed Prophet ﷺ urged Muslims to talk to one another; if there is some cause of anger between them, he said that they should not allow that anger to last more than three days, and the Muslim who is first to make up, first to give the greeting, will deserve a higher place before Allah ﷻ.

We should greet everyone, whether male, female, child, young or old, and whether we know them or do not know them. Whoever greets us we should respond warmly and fully. In general, we should be eager to give the greeting and try to be first to do so. Otherwise, it may help to observe the following guidelines:

1. To express respect, younger persons should greet their elders.
2. Someone walking should greet someone seated; similarly, someone riding should greet someone walking.
3. A smaller group should greet a larger group, and, whether in greeting or in response, one person can speak for the whole group if that is more convenient.

As always, some concrete examples of how the Blessed Prophet ﷺ acted, will best explain the principle and practice of true courtesy when greeting others:

One day, Zaid bin Harithah ﷺ who had just returned from a voyage, went to see the Blessed Prophet ﷺ, who immediately called him in and stood to receive him. The Blessed Prophet ﷺ had just taken off his shirt and a part of it was lying on his shoulders, the other end had slipped to the ground. He embraced Zaid and kissed his head.

Whenever Fatimah ﷺ, the youngest daughter of the Blessed Prophet ﷺ, came to him, he would stand up, kiss her on the head and, taking her hands, seat her beside himself.

Sa'd bin Mu'adh ﷺ, a respected Companion of the Blessed Prophet ﷺ, and a chief among his people, was made judge in a case and, although he had been wounded and had still not fully recovered, he came to the mosque to decide the case. The Blessed Prophet ﷺ saw him coming and asked the audience to stand up and receive their chief respectfully.

Abu Dharr ﷺ, another Companion, was sent for by the Blessed Prophet ﷺ, but was not at home. When later he returned home and was told of the Blessed Prophet's request he immediately rushed to see him. The Blessed Prophet ﷺ received him very cordially and embraced him.

These traditions tell us that in Islam it is proper to (i) show pleasure at the arrival of a guest and stand in respect to receive him; (ii) to embrace or shake hands with a guest; and (iii) to kiss a guest's head or forehead.

Visiting others

Again, the first principle is humility about oneself and consideration for the other person. In the matter of visiting the homes of others, this principle is expressed by honouring the privacy of the person visited and by remembering that he or she has the perfect right to refuse to let you in. So, the visitor should stand to one side of the entrance of the house and give the greeting. He may, after that, ask for permission to enter. It is clearly stated that if, after the third asking, permission is not granted, the visitor should leave. So important is it to give proper notice to the people inside a house, that a Muslim is advised, even when entering his own home, to give the greeting clearly and so, as it were, announce himself. It is never courteous to burst in on people.

Once inside, it is good manners for the Muslim to greet all persons in the house and ask after their good health. The visitor should not touch anything without the owner's permission. And he should ask permission before leaving the house at the end of the visit. If, during the visit, the host asks for help in any matter, the visitor should do his best to oblige.

One day the Blessed Prophet ﷺ called at the house of Sa'd bin 'Ubadah ﷺ, one of his Companions. He stood to one side of the door, and greeted Sa'd ﷺ. Sa'd responded to the greeting but in a very low voice and from inside the house. Qais, Sa'd's ﷺ son, saw that the Blessed Prophet ﷺ was at the door and asked his father to call him in. But Sa'd asked his son to keep quiet so that the Blessed Prophet ﷺ would greet him again. He said that a greeting from the Blessed Prophet ﷺ was a great blessing. The Blessed Prophet ﷺ then greeted him again and Sa'd again replied gently. The Blessed Prophet ﷺ greeted him for a third time and again Sa'd replied as before. After the third salutation the Blessed Prophet ﷺ turned to leave, but Sa'd ran after him and said: 'O Messenger of Allah ﷺ! My very life is pledged for you. I heard your greeting but wanted to hear the prayers (peace be upon you and Allah's mercy) from your lips. It is the greatest blessing for us and therefore I committed this act of arrogance. Kindly forgive me and grace my house.'

The Blessed Prophet ﷺ entered the house and, because it was a hot summer's day, Sa'd invited him to take a bath.

Sa'd then presented the Blessed Prophet ﷺ with a saffron robe, and the Blessed Prophet ﷺ prayed for prosperity and blessings on his host. Then Sa'd served food to him. After the meal, the Blessed Prophet ﷺ made ready to leave and Sa'd offered his horse and put a red sheet on its back. He then instructed his son to accompany the Blessed Prophet ﷺ and they set off with Qais walking by the side of the horse. After a short distance the Blessed Prophet ﷺ invited Qais to ride on the horse but Qais begged to be excused. The Blessed Prophet ﷺ then asked Qais to return home and, after saluting the Blessed Prophet ﷺ, Qais did so.

From this tradition we learn, among other things, that:

1. When visiting, we should stand to one side of the entrance and not in a position where we can see inside. Peeping into another's house has been strictly prohibited by the Blessed Prophet ﷺ.
2. As Muslim hosts, we should be attentive to our guest. The Blessed Prophet ﷺ said that a believer must extend the fullest hospitality to his guest that he can.
3. When the guest leaves we should accompany him for some distance.
4. If we have a means of transport that can be of use to our guest, we should place it at his disposal when he leaves.

The Blessed Prophet Muhammad ﷺ also said that we should give our full name if the person we are visiting asks for it; we should not say only 'it's me' or something else equally unhelpful.

Consideration for the host

The Blessed Prophet ﷺ advised against visiting the same person day after day, however close he may be. He told his Companion Abu Hurayrah ﷺ, for example, to visit him every other day, as this increases love and affection.

Calling too often or staying too long does not add to mutual affection. It may sometimes cause strain in a friendship. When a Muslim visits, he should choose a convenient time of day, and avoid mealtimes and times when his host may be resting or sleeping. If he must visit during such hours, he should try to call after meals so that the host is not burdened. However, if he has not eaten, he should not say that he has. *The Blessed Prophet ﷺ has commanded us not to combine hunger and falsehood. We may give some other reason for not eating.*

When visiting someone living in another town, we should inform him beforehand of the day and time of our arrival. It is not proper to arrive at someone's house without prior notice. It is quite possible that our host may be away or may have some urgent business; or he may be sick or there may be another reason why he cannot receive us or which would make our visit a nuisance to him.

Whenever the Blessed Prophet ﷺ returned from a journey, he would send a messenger ahead to Madinah to inform of his arrival. It is not desirable to arrive at anyone's house during the night. This applies even to one's own house. *The Blessed Prophet ﷺ always entered Madinah during the day-time. First he visited the mosque and said some nafl (voluntary) prayers, met and spoke* with his Companions and then walked to his house. If the caravan arrived in the evening, he would spend the night outside Madinah and enter the city in the morning.

It is a *Sunnah* to bring gifts for members of the family and friends, according to one's means.

Some other traditions

Once, when he stopped to break his journey, the Blessed Prophet ﷺ received a visit from Halimah ﷺ. There was no place to sit so the Blessed Prophet ﷺ spread a sheet on the ground for her to sit on. When her husband came the Blessed Prophet ﷺ seated him also by extending the sheet. When his foster-brother came the Blessed Prophet ﷺ stood up to receive him and seated him by his side.

On another occasion, the Blessed Prophet ﷺ was sitting in the mosque when a visitor came to see him. He called the visitor over to his seat and said: 'Please be seated here.' The visitor said: 'There is enough space and I will sit somewhere else. Please remain seated.' But the Blessed Prophet ﷺ said: 'No! Please sit here. You are my guest and it is binding on a Muslim to offer a place to a visitor.'

A man with a well-established reputation for rudeness expressed a desire to call upon the Blessed Prophet ﷺ. The Blessed Prophet ﷺ remarked: 'May Allah ﷻ help us. The whole family is fed up of it. Allah ﷻ alone knows why he has come.' When the man arrived, the Blessed Prophet ﷺ received him politely and talked to him warmly. 'A'ishah ﷺ heard the conversation from behind a curtain. When the man left, she said: 'O Messenger of Allah 🌸! After what you have said about him before he came, how could you receive him and talk to him in such a polite and warm manner?' The Blessed Prophet 🌸 replied: 'O 'A'ishah! His evil or good behaviour is with him (it's his responsibility). When he came to meet me, it was my duty to receive him politely and talk to him warmly. Otherwise I too would be called an ill- mannered and harsh fellow. It is really very bad for a believer to be called ill-mannered.'

These traditions tell us that:

1. When anyone calls on us, it is our duty to offer him a good seat whether we are at home or on a journey.
2. If we do not have any other suitable seat, then we should offer our visitor a seat by our side. Our visitor should not then feel that we have been lacking in respect.
3. A believer should stand up to receive a visitor.
4. Whether the visitor is good or bad, polite or rude, it is our duty to treat him politely and reply to him in a gentle tone.
5. The worst visitor is the one who has a reputation for being rough and ill-mannered. *The Blessed Prophet 🌸 said that the worst person is the one whom people are reluctant to meet because of his ill-mannered talk.*

We also know from the traditions that when a visitor was about to leave, the Blessed Prophet 🌸 would take his hands affectionately in his own, and pray for his safety, his faith and for good deeds from him.

Questions

1. How should we greet others?
2. In what sort of tone of voice should we speak to others?
3. Why should Muslims refrain from not speaking to each other for more than three days?
4. How did the Blessed Prophet ﷺ greet his daughter Fatimah ؉?
5. Who was Sa'd bin Mu'adh ؓ and what task was he given to perform?
6. How did the Blessed Prophet ﷺ ask that Sa'd bin Mu'adh ؓ be greeted?
7. How should we enter another's house?
8. What should we do if after asking three times we are not given permission to enter another's house?
9. How often did the Blessed Prophet ﷺ instruct one of his Companions to visit him?
10. At what times of day should we avoid visiting, and why?
11. Why did the Blessed Prophet ﷺ spend the night outside Madinah if he could not reach home during the day-time?
12. How should we receive someone who has a reputation for rudeness?
13. How should we welcome a guest, and how should we part from him?

- 9 -

Courtesies for Groups and Public Assemblies

Before going to any large gathering of people, in a school, mosque or any public meeting, we should first do *wudu* or have a full bath, put on clean clothes and, if possible, use perfume. *That was the practice of the Blessed Prophet* ﷺ *and he instructed all believers to do the same. On special occasions, and when meeting envoys from other countries, the Blessed Prophet* ﷺ *wore a special robe which he kept for that purpose.*

As we explained earlier, being clean is necessary to self-discipline and expresses a Muslim's sense of his dignity. Also, it shows respect and consideration for the other people who have to be physically near you, and respect for the occasion, the reason for your all being in the same place at the same time. That is why, for Friday prayers and for the two *'Id* festivals, taking a bath, wearing one's best clothes and some light perfume, are especially recommended. It is also recommended that a Muslim makes sure his breath does not smell bad. We should use a toothbrush (*miswak*), as the Blessed Prophet ﷺ did, every time we do *wudu*.

At any gathering, Muslims should make an effort not to form little gangs or cliques; it makes others feel left out. It is better to sit in a single large group instead. To crowd and squeeze against people is not good manners. When a visitor comes, space should be made for him so that he feels welcome. Where people have already gathered, it is rude to push past others to get to some particular spot in the meeting-place.

Often, at public meetings, spaces have to be reserved for those who are going to address the meeting, because it is easier for them to be seen and heard from there. It is common sense, as well as good manners, not to take such reserved places: it is embarrassing to have to be moved, and a nuisance for those arranging the meeting. Similarly, if the meeting is in someone's private house, it is arrogant to take his place, unless, of course, he offers it. To take anyone's place without permission or to make someone move, unless there is some very good reason, is seriously ill-mannered. The principle, as always, is to be humble about oneself and considerate of the needs and feelings of others.

It is inconsiderate, for instance, to sit between two persons obviously sitting together, unless invited. And it shows positive caring not to notice if someone has accidentally made some mistake in the way they speak or dress. If some people are clearly having a private conversation, it is considerate to not overhear. *The Blessed Prophet ﷺ said that he who listens to the private conversations of others will be punished on the Day of Judgement by having molten lead poured into his ears.*

We should be attentive at the meeting, keep in confidence what we hear in confidence, and share with others what all are meant to hear. It is inconsiderate to prevent others from attending to the business of the meeting by laughing and joking loudly or by coughing unceasingly. *The Blessed Prophet* 🕮 *himself never laughed out loud: in lighter moments he would only smile. It is rude to yawn; the Blessed Prophet* 🕮 *said we should cover the mouth to stifle a yawn and, if it could not be stifled, we should yawn without making a noise.* Sneezing can pass infections from one person to another: to prevent this happening, we should use the hand or a handkerchief. After sneezing a Muslim should say *alhamdulillah* ('Praise belongs to Allah 🕮') and any Muslim present should respond *yarhamukallah* ('Allah 🕮 bestow His mercy on you'), and the person who sneezed should acknowledge that prayer with *yahdikumullah wa yuslihu balakum* ('Allah 🕮 guide you and improve your condition'). If the person who sneezes is a non-Muslim, a Muslim should pray for his guidance and improvement.

If we attend some gathering where maybe time is wasted in worthless jokes and entertainment, we should afterward recite the following prayer: *Subhanaka Allahumma wa bi hamdika nashhadu an-la-ilaha illa anta, nastaghfiruka wa natubu ilaika* ('Blessed are You, O Allah! We praise You and witness that there is no god besides You. We turn to You for deliverance and we repent.')

On the public highway

The Blessed Prophet 🕮 *said: 'Do not sit by the roadside. if you have to sit there, observe the traditions. They are to*

*look downwards, not to cast evil glances at anyone, not
to harass anyone, and to remove stones, pieces of glass
and thorns so that others may not be injured. Assist the
needy, help those who are labouring, guide travellers,
prevent evil acts and encourage acts of piety.'*

Eating

The particular aims of the Muslim courtesies in eating
and drinking are: to help Muslims remember that they
owe their provisions to Allah ﷻ and so be grateful; to
want to share those blessings with others and so be
mindful of others' needs as well as their own; to observe
simple rules of cleanliness and decorum which make
eating healthy and beneficial for the individual and
community.

Because food is so obvious and necessary a blessing
from Allah ﷻ, it is vital for a Muslim to be conscious of
the fact. Both in preparing and eating food he should be
calm, orderly and respectful. Both actions should be
begun in Allah's name; if you forget to say Allah's name
when you begin, you should do so as soon as you
remember. Hands must be clean; so too, cooking pots,
serving dishes and plates.

It is wrong to throw food about in a light-hearted or
careless manner. It is wrong to lounge about or to lie
against cushions when eating. It is wrong to waste food;
if any falls on the ground, it should be picked up,
carefully cleaned and then eaten; only if that is
impossible should food be thrown away. It is a waste of

food to eat just for the sake of eating; a Muslim should eat to satisfy his hunger, no more.

A believing person should keep his diet simple; overly-rich, expensive foods are rarely healthy, being usually designed to tease the appetite, not satisfy it. A Muslim should stop eating while a little hunger remains. This is good for the body and its digestive system; it is also good for the spirit, because it practices self-control. *The Blessed Prophet* ﷺ *said that a few morsels are enough 'to keep the back straight'.* Of course we must eat to live, but eating is not the aim of life. *A believer, the Prophet* ﷺ *said, takes enough food to fill one intestine, while an unbeliever takes enough to fill seven.* Eating off gold or silver plates is forbidden to Muslims; money spent on such things is much better spent making sure others have enough to eat.

It is better to avoid eating alone. Food is from Allah ﷻ and should be shared. Eating with others is an occasion that brings people together and helps to form, and to improve, good relations. It really is true, *as the Blessed Prophet* ﷺ *said, that food for one is enough for two, food for two is enough for three,* and so on: in ordinary, everyday practice it is found that the will to share and the act of sharing make the amount of food sufficient for the people present; there is a physical satisfaction that comes from sharing, and the hunger of the body is satisfied within that. It is insincerity in the willingness to share that changes a normal, healthy appetite into a raging fire which then burns up the food and so makes it insufficient.

The usual rules of consideration for others apply when eating in company. Unless there is an urgent reason for doing otherwise, food should be offered to the oldest first, this is a mark of respect, and passed round to the right. A Muslim should put food in his mouth with his right hand, eating slowly and calmly. It is good to praise the food in a moderate way to show appreciation to the host and to the person who cooked it. To say that the food is too salty or not salty enough is permitted; but it is not good to criticize the food itself.

When food is taken from a common dish, you should not either use your hand, or allow anything to fall into it, in such a way that others present cannot then serve them-selves from it. He should only dip his fingers into his food to the extent necessary, and not greedily thrust in his whole hand: *the Blessed Prophet* ﷺ *generally used the thumb and two fingers only.* If the food is too hot, you should wait for it to cool; breathing on it to cool it quickly is not hygienic.

A Muslim should be careful during mealtimes not to talk about things that might put others off their food.

At the end of the meal, hands should be washed and dried, and a Muslim should express thanks to Allah ﷻ. All left-over food should be cleared away as soon as practicable: leaving food unattended is disrespectful. If you have been a guest at the meal, it is good to say a prayer for the well-being and prosperity of your host, in addition to thanking him.

Drinking

The courtesies when drinking are very similar to those to be observed when eating. We should make sure that the water-container and the water are clean, and use the right hand for both serving and drinking. We should sit rather than stand, and drink slowly and in moderation. After finishing, we should thank Allah 🕮, and cover the water-container carefully. *The Blessed Prophet 🕮 prohibited breathing into the water container:* the reasons are obvious. As when eating, the use of gold and silver utensils is forbidden. When serving others we should pass the water to the person on our right, who will also pass it to his right. The container will eventually return to us when we may then drink from it ourselves. Milk is an especially wholesome and nourishing drink; for that reason, to be conscious of and grateful for its benefits, a Muslim should say a special prayer: *'O Allah! Bless us with it and increase it for us.'*

Dress and ornaments

Sadly, people often use clothes and ornaments as a way of making an impression on others, sometimes even of showing off their wealth or social position. Islam disapproves of these attitudes. The best ornament for a Muslim is his or her good character, expressed in knowledge and action. Of course, clothes do express a person's dignity and self-respect. Therefore, a Muslim should be careful about dress. But clothes that show vanity or vulgarity and expensive clothes for pride are prohibited in Islam, likewise clothes containing threads of real gold or silver. Muslim men are recommended not to wear brightly coloured clothes.

Cleanliness is of the greatest importance, but that does not mean clothes have to be new. We should not think of worn clothes as bad. The Blessed Prophet ﷺ and his Companions sometimes wore such clothes. *Even the two garments worn by the Blessed Prophet ﷺ at the time of his death were patched.* If by the grace of Allah ﷻ we can afford to put on new clothes, then we should say a prayer of thanks, and, as a practical way of expressing our gratitude to Allah ﷻ, give our old garments to whoever may need them.

Covering the body is one of the functions of clothes, and not one to forget, especially when praying, and also whenever we are seen in public. This applies to both Muslim men and Muslim women. For women, the clothes should not be so transparent and tight that the shape of the body is visible. *The Blessed Prophet ﷺ, when he dressed, put on clothes and shoes from the right, and took them off from the left.*

As for ornaments, men are allowed only a single silver ring, and though women are allowed ornaments of silver and gold, these were not liked by the Blessed Prophet Muhammad ﷺ, *who discouraged the wearing of all metal ornaments. Fatimah ﷺ was the Blessed Prophet's youngest daughter and his favourite child. He loved her so much that before he went on a journey and on his return he used to visit her. One day he saw that Fatimah ﷺ was wearing a gold necklace and this made him unhappy.*

When Fatimah ﷠ became aware of the Blessed Prophet's displeasure, she sold the necklace and gave the money as charity in the name of Allah ﷻ. When the Blessed Prophet ﷺ heard of Fatimah's good action, he thanked Allah ﷻ.

It is also related that once, when 'A'ishah ﷠ showed the Blessed Prophet ﷺ a golden bracelet, he advised her to change it for silver and have it coloured with saffron.

Questions

1. How should we prepare for public gatherings, marriage parties, etc?
2. Why is it better to avoid forming small groups on such occasions?
3. How will those who eavesdrop on private conversations be treated on the Day of Judgement?
4. What can we do to avoid annoying others when eating?
5. What actions show that we respect and are grateful for the blessings of food and drink?
6. Why does Islam disapprove of expensive clothes?
7. What kinds of clothes are prohibited in Islam?
8. From which side did the Blessed Prophet ﷺ put on clothes and shoes?
9. What did Fatimah ﷠ do when the Blessed Prophet ﷺ disapproved of her wearing a gold necklace?

- 10 -

Games and Sports

Throughout Islamic history physical training and sports have been encouraged in Islam. Muslims have an obligation to establish a healthy society by attending to both the physical and moral well-being of its members.

While attending to physical needs, however, certain constraints have to be observed. One should not go so far in satisfying the needs of the body that the person becomes uncaring about others and, along with that, forgetful of Allah ﷻ.

For Muslims, it is right and important to satisfy the needs of the body and, while doing so, to remember Allah ﷻ and thank Him. A part of that is looking after the body and making a positive effort to be healthy. To achieve this, a healthy diet and healthy exercise are essential. Games and sports are, if done in the right spirit, an excellent way of getting healthy exercise. The Blessed Prophet ﷺ himself engaged in certain sports and encouraged us to do the same.

Fencing, archery, javelin-throwing, are sports that teach balance, strength, grace, and the co-ordination of hand

and eye, as well as concentration and timing. Gymnastics, riding (horse or bicycle), wrestling are among sports that improve strength and stamina, and involve the training of most muscles in the body. Swimming, a sport highly commended by the Blessed Prophet ﷺ, uses every muscle in the body in a most balanced way, at the same time developing the lungs. Of course, in every sport, it is important to keep safety in mind, other people's as well as one's own. It is important that we observe the correct manner of dressing and keep our dignity at all times even in the changing rooms. Communal showers which are usually taken after swimming and sports are not in the Islamic spirit of decency and modesty.

We may and should take part in team games such as: orienteering, cricket and football are modern examples. *In the time of the Blessed Prophet ﷺ, Muslims gave demonstrations of some sports on 'Id days and the Blessed Prophet ﷺ and his Companions ﷺ enjoyed them. Once, some Africans gave a demonstration of lance work in the courtyard of the mosque in Madinah, watched by the Blessed Prophet ﷺ and his wife 'A'ishah ﷺ.*

A story about the Companions of the Blessed Prophet ﷺ will demonstrate how useful to the community skill in sports can be, in this case skill in archery and wrestling. *Preparations were under way for a battle and the Blessed Prophet's Companions were flocking to enlist. Boys of tender age, though eager to join, were not being recruited. One boy named Rafi' ﷺ was only fourteen but quite skilled at archery. His father recommended him to the Blessed Prophet ﷺ who allowed him to enlist. Another boy, named Samurah ﷺ, pleaded that he also should be* recruited, as he was stronger than Rafi' and could knock him down in wrestling. Samurah's father supported his claim, so the Blessed Prophet ﷺ ordered a wrestling match between the two boys. When Samurah ﷺ defeated Rafi' ﷺ, the Prophet ﷺ permitted him to enlist also. So Rafi' and Samurah ﷺ earned honour both in this world and in the next, because their strength and skill enabled them to serve the cause of Islam in battle.

'A'ishah ﷺ reported: The Prophet ﷺ was standing at the door of my room when the Abyssinians were playing with spears in the Mosque compound and Allah's Messenger ﷺ was covering me with his cloak in order that I might look over his shoulder at their sport. He would then stand there for my sake till I was the one who departed. Once when she was with Allah's Messenger ﷺ on a journey she raced him on foot and won but when she later put on some weight she raced him and he won. He said this makes up for that beating.

In another narration Abu Hurayrah ﷺ reported: While some Abyssinians were playing in the presence of the Prophet ﷺ, 'Umar ﷺ came in, picked up a pebble and hit them with it. The Prophet ﷺ said: O 'Umar! let them (to play).This was inside the mosque.

Certain games and sports are strictly forbidden. Games that involve pure chance, gambling or betting are prohibited. Games like these get people worked up to such a mental state that they are no longer able to control themselves, whether winning or losing, and cannot stop playing. It is for similar reasons that, in Islam, alcohol is forbidden; because it creates the sort of habit that people cannot control and on account of which they do terrible things to others as well as to themselves. Also forbidden are games and sports that can cause injury or harm to others; likewise games that can cause pain or harm to animals (bull fights, cock-fighting, bear-baiting, etc.) or which use animals as targets. Forbidden too are games that involve using bad words and which, if you play them, cause bad habits like unnecessary harshness or violence towards other people.

Aside from these sorts of sports and games, there are many pastimes which, because they invite and encourage people to waste time and resources are strongly disapproved. Firework displays, sometimes staged at marriages and on other such occasions, are a wild extravagance. People are often injured by the fireworks, property damaged and quite innocent small animals are pointlessly and cruelly terrified, sometimes even killed. Those who regularly go in for such activities are called 'brothers of the devil' in the Qur'an, because, instead of turning their time and resources into benefits for their fellow-creatures, they waste those resources and make them a means of injury or misery, which is the aim of the devil.

Cinema, clubbing, bhangras, music concerts, theatre, dancing, variety shows and TV programmes such as violent films, late-night movies, etc. should be avoided, as they destroy a person's sense of modesty and chastity, and encourage forgetfulness of Allah ﷻ which, in turn, inevitably leads to bad habits and selfishness.

Questions

1. How do games and sports contribute to the health of the body?
2. Give two examples of healthy activities.
3. How did skill in wrestling and archery help two young Muslims to join the army of the Blessed Prophet ﷺ?
4. Give two examples of prohibited games, and explain why they are prohibited.
5. Name two activities which encourage time-wasting and wasting of money, and forgetfulness of Allah ﷻ.

- 11 -

Promoting Unity, and
other Virtues

Promoting unity

Unity means being together, being as one: for Muslims,
unity means keeping up good relations with each other,
helping each other in need, and generally being peaceable.
Disunity means always quarrelling and looking for causes
to disagree about, and not helping each other in need. The
Qur'an clearly commands Muslims to be united:

$$\text{وَٱعْتَصِمُوا۟ بِحَبْلِ ٱللَّهِ جَمِيعًا وَلَا تَفَرَّقُوا۟}$$

*And hold steady, all of you together, to the rope of
Allah, and do not separate.* [Al 'Imran 3: 103]

$$\text{وَأَطِيعُوا۟ ٱللَّهَ وَرَسُولَهُۥ وَلَا تَنَـٰزَعُوا۟ فَتَفْشَلُوا۟ وَتَذْهَبَ}$$
$$\text{رِيحُكُمْ ۖ وَٱصْبِرُوٓا۟ ۚ إِنَّ ٱللَّهَ مَعَ ٱلصَّـٰبِرِينَ ﴿٤٦﴾}$$

*And obey Allah and His Messenger, and do not
quarrel with one another, or you will stumble and*

your strength go away from you. Rather, stand firm. Truly Allah is with those who stand firm. [al-Anfal 8: 46]

The institution of *salah* offers a way for Muslims of a locality to meet with each other five times a day in the local mosque. The obligatory congregational prayer on Friday is an opportunity for the Muslims of a whole town to gather in a single mosque for a single purpose, to praise Allah 🕮. For the two *'Id* prayers, Muslims from a still wider area have a chance to meet and celebrate together.

Above all, there is the institution of *hajj*, the pilgrimage to Makkah. It is an obligation on every Muslim, male or female, to make this pilgrimage once in a lifetime at least, if he or she has the means. Because of the *hajj* every Muslim knows that there is a wide world of Muslims of different races and colours and cultures and languages, beyond the small world of his own village or town. The chance to see and meet different people in this way, and for such a noble purpose, enriches the spirit with a practical example of brotherly unity among very diverse people, rich, poor, young, old, black, white, brown, yellow, all standing together, shoulder to shoulder, a single kinship under the One Allah 🕮.

The Blessed Prophet 🕮 said: 'All Muslims are like the bricks of a building that support each other.' Unity is of great practical importance, because it gives a community strength. Families, nations and countries that are united, enjoy a high reputation in the world, and move with confidence along the path of progress and prosperity. By contrast, disunited people are very vulnerable to defeat and humiliation at the hands of their enemies and lose the strength necessary to run their own affairs.

Thus, it is every Muslim's duty:

1. to express solidarity with other Muslims and develop unity of purpose and action;
2. to avoid actions that create differences and disputes;
3. to never quarrel with anyone, and if he does, to reconcile immediately and keep his heart free of bitterness and hate;
4. to do every major piece of work after proper consultation with and, so far as possible, with the consent of, all those who are concerned or affected by it;
5. not to differ with the advice of others just for the sake of it, just to stick to his own point of view;
6. to join the congregation on Fridays in a *Jami'* mosque;
7. to attend the two *'Id* prayers and celebrate in company with others;
8. whenever he prays with others, to keep the rows of worshippers straight: the Blessed Prophet ﷺ said that deviation from this practice affects the heart and leads to differences among Muslims;
9. to appreciate others' good deeds and overlook their shortcomings.

Putting others first, showing respect and kindness, being open and generous and eager to share: these are the attributes that help to unify Muslims. *The Blessed Prophet ﷺ said to his Companions: 'Listen, I will tell you a thing that is better than voluntary prayers, fasting, giving alms, and charity. What is it? It is to strive to remove social evils and make up differences and quarrels.' Then he added: 'Take note. To develop differences in society is just like (making) a razor which, instead of hair, shaves off faith.'*

Avoiding distrust

Distrust is a root cause of difficult relations, in turn the root of many evils, and is therefore an attitude prohibited to Muslims. It is a fact of ordinary experience that a person imagines others to be like himself. A good person thinks others good, while an evil person suspects others of being evil too. Those who were used to looking to selfish interests and worldly gain could never imagine that the unbelievers of Makkah would embrace Islam: they thought that the Blessed Prophet ﷺ was preaching for his own benefit and not for them. *The Blessed Prophet ﷺ said: 'The worst lie is to distrust somebody.'*

Distrusting others is often worse than saying outright that they are lying. This is because we will investigate what we believe to be a lie, and it often turns out that it was not, in fact, any lie. This process can increase unity. But when we are merely suspicious about someone, we often do not take the trouble to check up, and the suspicion grows into a fire of anger and enmity that may easily burn up friendship and unity. Both the Qur'an and *Sunnah* stress that we should not let distrust grow, that we should exercise the utmost care in forming opinions about others.

Distrust in the heart tempts one to look for the worst in others, and though we do not find it, we continue to expect some fault. Only the Prophets are immune from sin. All other human beings, including great scholars and saints, have some weaknesses. But if some suspicion about a person, especially a famous person, takes hold, people turn away from him, or take no notice of his advice or judgement; indeed, in such a situation, people may start taking sides, form opposing groups or parties, and, instead of unity among Muslims, disputes and wars can result.

The Blessed Prophet ﷺ said: 'Do not try to find fault in others.' And: 'If you persist in finding faults in others you are sure to quarrel with each other.' Anyone who looks for faults in his Muslim brother, Allah ﷻ will expose his hidden vices, and then nothing can conceal them.

Another side to distrust is the fact that it does not allow people to accept the reasons given by the person suspected. They always consider that he is 'only' making excuses for himself. It is a great sin not to listen sympathetically to the explanations of his actions offered by someone in his own defence.

The Blessed Prophet ﷺ said: 'Anyone who does not accept the explanation or defence given by his brother is a great tyrant. Always remember to look for and appreciate the virtues of others and overlook their shortcomings.' That indeed is the basic principle of unity in collective life.

Controlling anger

A Muslim should show sympathy for others' distress, even his worst enemies. *The Blessed Prophet ﷺ said: 'Never be happy at the misery of your brother. Be afraid in case Allah ﷻ is merciful to him and takes hold of you.'* To show anger, to taunt, to abuse are not qualities expected of a believer. It is the duty of a Muslim rather to refrain from all these. *'Anger,' the Blessed Prophet ﷺ said, 'undoes faith, just as sibr (an extremely bitter fruit) undoes honey.' He also said: 'A man does not deserve to be called brave if he gets the better of a wrestler in a bout. A really brave person is the one who gets the better of his temper.'*

A man said to the Blessed Prophet ﷺ: 'O Messenger of Allah ﷻ! Please give me some small advice that I will be able to follow.' The Blessed Prophet ﷺ said: 'Do not show your temper.' The man put the same question two or three times more but got the same answer. The Blessed Prophet ﷺ also declared: 'One who taunts, curses, hurls abuse or talks rudely is not a believer.' And: 'Abusing is a sin and quarrels lead to lack of faith.' He also said: 'O Muslims, do not pick faults in others. Do not cheat. Do not be jealous of each other. Do not be nasty or indulge in back-biting. Servants of Allah ﷻ, live as brothers to one another.'

So, if in our affairs with others, we feel angry, we should control our anger and forgive. The command of the Qur'an in this matter is quite clear:

وَأَطِيعُوا۟ ٱللَّهَ وَٱلرَّسُولَ لَعَلَّكُمْ تُرْحَمُونَ ﴿١٣٢﴾ ۞ وَسَارِعُوٓا۟ إِلَىٰ مَغْفِرَةٍ
مِّن رَّبِّكُمْ وَجَنَّةٍ عَرْضُهَا ٱلسَّمَٰوَٰتُ وَٱلْأَرْضُ أُعِدَّتْ لِلْمُتَّقِينَ ﴿١٣٣﴾ ٱلَّذِينَ
يُنفِقُونَ فِى ٱلسَّرَّآءِ وَٱلضَّرَّآءِ وَٱلْكَٰظِمِينَ ٱلْغَيْظَ وَٱلْعَافِينَ عَنِ ٱلنَّاسِ
وَٱللَّهُ يُحِبُّ ٱلْمُحْسِنِينَ ﴿١٣٤﴾

And obey Allah and the Messenger, so that you may find mercy. And compete with each other for forgiveness from your Lord, and for a paradise as wide as the heavens and the earth, ready for those who push back (evil); ready for those who spend in time of ease and time of hardship (from what Allah ﷻ has given them); ready for those who control their anger and are forgiving toward their fellow men. Allah ﷻ loves the good.

[Al 'Imran 3: 132-4]

The Blessed Prophet ﷺ gave some practical advice about how to achieve self-control. First, we can do it by praying to Allah ﷻ; then, if we are standing at the time, by sitting down, or by lying down if we are sitting at the time. Once, when 'Urwah, a Companion of the Blessed Prophet ﷺ, lost his temper, he started doing *wudu* with water. He explained that the Blessed Prophet ﷺ had described anger to him as an act of the devil who is made of fire, and fire is extinguished by water. Thus, when we feel anger, we can put out its fire by doing *wudu*. Another way of dispelling our anger is to drink some water. Also, to be secure against the after-effects of anger, we should make up for anything said or done as soon as our anger has subsided.

It is advisable to be the first to give the greeting to end a dispute. *The Blessed Prophet* 🕌 *said; 'The best among you is the one who salutes first.' If the other person responds, he will get equal reward, but if he does not, he will be liable to punishment.* If the quarrelling persons are not themselves able to resume friendly relations, others may mediate between them. It has been narrated that arbitration is better for the spirit than voluntary prayers and fasting. The person mediating between quarrelling parties can bring them together even by with-holding a part of the truth, if that helps to achieve a genuine reconciliation: such a person should not be called a liar, *the Blessed Prophet* 🕌 *said, because bringing Muslims together is a most noble motive.*

Honesty and dishonesty

To keep intact what you have been entrusted with, and deliver it back to the rightful owner at the appointed time, is honesty. Whatever Allah 🕌 has given to any of His servants is given to that person in trust and he should discharge that trust according to Allah's wishes. Not to do so is dishonest. For example, the ears are a trust and should not be used to hear things disliked by Allah 🕌; the tongue should not be used to pronounce undesirable things, and so on.

Ibrahim bin Ad'ham, may Allah have mercy on him, a saintly man, was renowned for his devotion to the All-Mighty Allah 🕌. To earn a living he accepted the post of watchman of an orchard. One day the owner came to the orchard and asked Ibrahim to bring him a sweet pomegranate. But the pomegranate Ibrahim brought him turned out to be sour. The owner then asked him to bring another, but it too turned out to be sour. The owner became angry and asked Ibrahim why he did not bring him a sweet fruit. Ibrahim said that he did not know the inner state of the fruit, only its outward appearance. The owner said to him that, being the watchman he should know which fruits were sweet. Ibrahim explained that he had been entrusted to watch over the garden, not to taste the fruits, and therefore could not know which were sweet.

The owner was so delighted when he heard this that he increased Ibrahim's wages, but Ibrahim, may Allah have mercy on him, left the job, saying that he did not wish to be paid for his honesty.

The Blessed Prophet ﷺ compared a dishonest person to a hypocrite. He also said: 'A dishonest person does not have any faith.'

Questions

1. How do *salah*, the two *'Id* prayers, and *hajj* help to unify Muslims?
2. Can you name seven things a Muslim should do, and two he should not do, to help promote Muslim unity?
3. Why is suspecting a fellow-Muslim sometimes worse than accusing him outright?
4. What are some ways of overcoming one's anger and keeping self-control?
5. Honesty is discharging a trust that you have been given fully and faithfully. Can you give some examples of it?

- 12 -

Racial and Colour Equality

In the sight of Allah ﷻ no man is automatically superior to another man, nor is any race superior to any other. Allah ﷻ shows His Mercy sometimes to white people and sometimes to non-white. All, black or white or brown or red or yellow, all are His people, all descendants of Adam, peace be upon him. Raised in Allah's eyes are only those who are most fearful of Him and who are best in conduct:

يَٰٓأَيُّهَا ٱلنَّاسُ إِنَّا خَلَقْنَٰكُم مِّن ذَكَرٍ وَأُنثَىٰ وَجَعَلْنَٰكُمْ شُعُوبًا وَقَبَآئِلَ لِتَعَارَفُوٓا۟ إِنَّ أَكْرَمَكُمْ عِندَ ٱللَّهِ أَتْقَىٰكُمْ إِنَّ ٱللَّهَ عَلِيمٌ خَبِيرٌ ﴿١٣﴾

O mankind! We have created you male and female, and have made you nations and tribes so that you could distinguish one from another. The noblest of you in the sight of Allah is the best in conduct. Verily, Allah is All-Knowing, All-Aware. [al-Hujurat 49: 13]

The Blessed Prophet ﷺ said: 'O mankind, your God is one and you have but one father. You are all progeny of Adam, and Adam was made of clay. Lo! The noblest among you, in the sight of Allah is the best in conduct. No Arab has any superiority over a non-Arab save by his piety.'

'Uqbah b. 'Amir ﷺ reported Allah's Messenger ﷺ as saying: *'These genealogies of yours are not a cause of reviling anyone. You are all sons of Adam [that all men, being descended from the one ancestor]. No one has superiority over another except in religion and piety. It is enough reproach for a man to be foul, obscene and niggardly.'*

Sa'id ibn Musayyib, may Allah have mercy on him, was a very great and famous scholar. He was the leader of the *tabi'in*, those who succeeded the Companions, may Allah be pleased with all of them. An African once visited him and, perhaps because he was a stranger, hesitated to ask Sa'id what he had come to ask him. When Sa'id realized this, he said: 'Don't be hesitant on account of your colour. Among Allah's foremost servants were three dark-skinned men: Bilal ﷺ, the first *mu'adhdhin*, who most faithfully served the Blessed Prophet ﷺ; Mehjan, who was the attendant of 'Umar al-Faruq ﷺ; and Luqman ﷺ the Wise, who was an African.'

Luqman used to address people in small gatherings and give them good advice. Later, an old friend of his, much to his surprise, saw Luqman addressing a huge gathering. He asked him: 'Are you not the same man, the shepherd who used to graze goats? How did you attain such a position as this?' Luqman replied: 'I tell the truth and avoid uselessness.'

It is also narrated that a man came to see Luqman and said: 'Luqman, you were once someone's servant. You used to be my shepherd. And you are a dark-skinned man . . .' Luqman asked him: 'My blackness is obvious, but tell me, what is it about me that has struck you?' The man replied: 'I have seen people coming to you in all humility and showing you respect and they were pleased with your sermon.' Luqman explained: 'Listen, if you do the same things I do, then you will be like me!' 'What things are those?' asked the man. Luqman said: 'I lower my gaze, control my tongue, honour my guest, take care of my neighbour, and avoid all useless things in life. These are a few things that have elevated me to my present position.'

About Luqman, a renowned Companion, Abu Darda' ﷺ, said: 'Luqman was neither very rich, nor had a very elevated family background, nor had many children to be proud of. He had an average personality and was a quiet and reasonable man who had a penetrating insight into matters. He never slept in the day, nobody saw him coughing, spitting, urinating, or bathing in public, or taking part in amusements, and nobody heard him laughing aloud. Whenever he spoke, he spoke wisdom. He used to visit rulers and administrators, to ponder on their affairs, and he drew lessons from this.'

Such facts about Luqman are recorded in history, but he is renowned above all because Allah ﷻ has mentioned his name in His Book, and named a *surah* after him. Allah ﷻ, says very clearly in the Qur'an that he gave Luqman wisdom. Luqman gave some advice to his son which is recorded in the Qur'an and which applies to every child of the Muslim community. Parents should take special note of it and should give such advice to their children, and pray to obtain such blessings.

Questions

1. Explain why Allah ﷻ created human-beings in different colour and racial groups?
2. Name three men of African origin who earned great status in society and give an example of their qualities.
3. Describe how Islam emphasises respect for all of the human race in general.
4. On what criteria does Allah ﷻ judge mankind?
5. For what quality is Luqman praised in the Qur'an?
6. What do we know of how Luqman behaved?
7. What does Islam teach about equality of human-beings?

Luqman's Advice
to His Son

بِسْمِ ٱللَّهِ ٱلرَّحْمَٰنِ ٱلرَّحِيمِ

وَلَقَدْ ءَاتَيْنَا لُقْمَٰنَ ٱلْحِكْمَةَ أَنِ ٱشْكُرْ لِلَّهِ وَمَن يَشْكُرْ فَإِنَّمَا يَشْكُرُ لِنَفْسِهِ

وَمَن كَفَرَ فَإِنَّ ٱللَّهَ غَنِيٌّ حَمِيدٌ ۞ وَإِذْ قَالَ لُقْمَٰنُ لِٱبْنِهِ وَهُوَ يَعِظُهُ يَٰبُنَيَّ لَا تُشْرِكْ بِٱللَّهِ

إِنَّ ٱلشِّرْكَ لَظُلْمٌ عَظِيمٌ ۞

وَوَصَّيْنَا ٱلْإِنسَٰنَ بِوَٰلِدَيْهِ حَمَلَتْهُ أُمُّهُ وَهْنًا عَلَىٰ وَهْنٍ وَفِصَٰلُهُۥ فِي عَامَيْنِ

أَنِ ٱشْكُرْ لِي وَلِوَٰلِدَيْكَ إِلَيَّ ٱلْمَصِيرُ ۞ وَإِن جَٰهَدَاكَ عَلَىٰٓ أَن تُشْرِكَ بِي مَا لَيْسَ

لَكَ بِهِۦ عِلْمٌ فَلَا تُطِعْهُمَا وَصَاحِبْهُمَا فِي ٱلدُّنْيَا مَعْرُوفًا وَٱتَّبِعْ سَبِيلَ مَنْ أَنَابَ إِلَيَّ

ثُمَّ إِلَيَّ مَرْجِعُكُمْ فَأُنَبِّئُكُم بِمَا كُنتُمْ تَعْمَلُونَ ۞

يَٰبُنَيَّ إِنَّهَآ إِن تَكُ مِثْقَالَ حَبَّةٍ مِّنْ خَرْدَلٍ فَتَكُن فِي صَخْرَةٍ أَوْ فِي ٱلسَّمَٰوَٰتِ

أَوْ فِي ٱلْأَرْضِ يَأْتِ بِهَا ٱللَّهُ إِنَّ ٱللَّهَ لَطِيفٌ خَبِيرٌ ۞ يَٰبُنَيَّ أَقِمِ ٱلصَّلَوٰةَ وَأْمُرْ

بِٱلْمَعْرُوفِ وَٱنْهَ عَنِ ٱلْمُنكَرِ وَٱصْبِرْ عَلَىٰ مَآ أَصَابَكَ إِنَّ ذَٰلِكَ مِنْ عَزْمِ ٱلْأُمُورِ ۞

وَلَا تُصَعِّرْ خَدَّكَ لِلنَّاسِ وَلَا تَمْشِ فِي ٱلْأَرْضِ مَرَحًا إِنَّ ٱللَّهَ لَا يُحِبُّ كُلَّ مُخْتَالٍ فَخُورٍ ۞

وَٱقْصِدْ فِي مَشْيِكَ وَٱغْضُضْ مِن صَوْتِكَ إِنَّ أَنكَرَ ٱلْأَصْوَٰتِ لَصَوْتُ ٱلْحَمِيرِ ۞

In the name of Allah, the Merciful, the Mercy-Giving.

And truly We gave Luqman wisdom, saying: 'Give thanks to Allah and whoever gives thanks, he does so for (the betterment of) his soul. And whoever refuses, Allah is Absolute, the Owner of Praise.'

And (remember) what Luqman said to his son, when he was advising him: 'My dear son! Never associate partners with Allah. Indeed joining partners with Allah (shirk) is the highest wrong-doing.'

And [Allah says] We have enjoined on man (to be dutiful and good) to his parent. His mother bore him by bearing strain upon strain, and his utter dependence on her lasted two years: [hence, O man] be grateful towards your parent, [and remember that] to Me is all journey's end. [Revere your parent] yet should they endeavour to make you join in worship with Me others that of which you have no knowledge, then obey them not [but even then] bear them company in this world's life with kindness, and follow the path of those who turn to Me in repentance and obedience. In the end, unto Me you all must return and thereupon I shall tell you all that you were doing.

'My dear son, [continued Luqman] listen! Even if it is something as small as the weight of a grain of mustard seed, and though it is inside a rock, or in the heavens, or in the earth, Allah will bring it out. Allah is Subtle, All-Aware.

My dear son! Establish prayer and command kindness and forbid evil, and persevere whatever may happen to you. (To do) that is of the steady and firm heart of things.

Do not turn your cheek in scorn to people; and do not walk conceitedly in the land. Allah does not love anyone who brags or shows off.

Be modest in your bearing and keep your voice down. The harshest of all voices is the voice of the ass!' [Luqman 31: 12-19]

-14-

Purity, Modesty and Chastity

Purity, modesty and chastity are part of Islamic morals and manners. Islam begins from purity of belief. That is belief in the oneness of God and cleansing oneself from all sorts of atheistic and polytheistic beliefs and practices. One also has to cleanse his thoughts from thinking ill of others, jealousy, hatred, etc. And after that purity and cleanliness of the body is also important. As Allah ﷻ says:

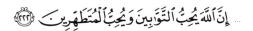

... Surely Allah loves those who turn to Allah in repentance and those who purify themselves. [Al-Baqarah 2: 222]

The Blessed Prophet ﷺ said: *'Purity is half of faith.'*

Modesty and shyness is greatly emphasized in Islam as our beloved Prophet ﷺ said: *'Every religion has a special kind of morality and Islam's special morality is modesty and shyness.'*

The Blessed Prophet ﷺ also said: *'What the people have inherited from the previous prophecies is the statement that if you are not modest and feel no shame then do as you wish.'* This means that the quality of modesty and shyness or shame prevents a person from indulging in all sorts of bad behaviour.

Chastity is a quality which has been encouraged by Islam. Allah ﷻ says:

وَٱلۡحَٰفِظِينَ فُرُوجَهُمۡ وَٱلۡحَٰفِظَٰتِ وَٱلذَّٰكِرِينَ ٱللَّهَ كَثِيرًا
وَٱلذَّٰكِرَٰتِ أَعَدَّ ٱللَّهُ لَهُم مَّغۡفِرَةً وَأَجۡرًا عَظِيمًا ﴿٣٥﴾

... For men and women who guard their chastity, and for men and women who engage much in Allah's praise; – For them has Allah prepared forgiveness and great reward. [Al-Ahzab 33: 35]

The Blessed Prophet ﷺ said: *'Those who give me the guarantee of guarding that which lies between the two thighs (chastity) and also that lying between their two jaws (the tongue), I shall guarantee Paradise for them.'*

A frequent supplication of the Blessed Prophet ﷺ was: *'O Allah, I ask You for good guidance, for piety and chastity and being independent of all except You.'*

A final word

In concluding this book, there are four *ahadith* of the Blessed Prophet ﷺ which according to some great *imams* form the essence of the Islamic moral system and from which most of the details are drawn. They are very easy to remember and should be reflected upon in all spheres of life. These *ahadith* are as follows:

عَنْ قَتَادَةَ ﷺ قَالَ قَالَ رَسُولُ اللهِ ﷺ :

"لاَ يُؤْمِنُ أَحَدُكُمْ حَتَّى يُحِبَّ لِلنَّاسِ مَا يُحِبُّ لِنَفْسِهِ" (رواه أحمد)

Qatadah ﷺ narrated: Allah's Messenger ﷺ said: 'No one is a proper believer until he likes for the people what he likes for himself.'

عَنْ أَبِي هُرَيْرَةَ ﷺ قَالَ قَالَ رَسُولُ اللهِ ﷺ :

"مَنْ كَانَ يُؤْمِنُ بِاللهِ وَالْيَوْمِ الآخِرِ فَلْيَقُلْ خَيْراً أَوْ لِيَصْمُتْ" (رواه البخاري)

Abu Hurayrah ﷺ reported: The Messenger of Allah ﷺ said: 'Whoever believes in Allah and the Day of Judgement, either speak good or keep silent.'

عَنْ أَبِي هُرَيْرَةَ رَضِيَ اللهُ أَنَّ رَجُلاً قَالَ لِلنَّبِيِّ ﷺ : "أَوْصِنِي" فَقَالَ ﷺ

"لاَ تَغْضَبْ، فَرَدَّدَ ذَلِكَ مِرَاراً، قَالَ لاَ تَغْضَبْ" (رواه البخاري)

Abu Hurayrah ﷺ said: A man said to the Prophet ﷺ: 'Please give me special advice.' The Prophet ﷺ said: 'Do not become angry (do not lose your temper)' The man repeated his request several times and the Prophet ﷺ gave, again and again, the same advice 'Do not become angry.'

عَنْ أَبِي هُرَيْرَةَ ﷺ قَالَ قَالَ رَسُولُ اللهِ ﷺ :

"مِنْ حُسْنِ إِسْلاَمِ الْمَرْءِ تَرْكُهُ مَا لاَ يَعْنِيهِ" (رواه البخاري)

It is also reported by Abu Hurayrah ﷺ that the Blessed Prophet ﷺ said: 'Part of someone's being a good Muslim is that he leaves alone what does not concern him.'

Honorific Titles

1.	*Subḥānahū wa Ta'ālā* Glorified and Exalted is He	سُبْحَانَهُ وَتَعَالَى
2.	*Ṣallallāhu 'alaihi wa sallam* May Allah bless him and grant him peace	صَلَّى اللهُ عَلَيْهِ وَسَلَّم
3.	*'Alayhis salām* Peace be upon him	عَلَيْهِ السَّلاَم
4.	*Raḍiyallāhu 'anhu* May Allah be pleased with him	رَضِيَ اللهُ عَنْهُ
5.	*Raḍiyallāhu 'anhumā* May Allah be pleased with them both	رَضِيَ اللهُ عَنْهُمَا
6.	*Raḍiyallāhu 'anhum* May Allah be pleased with them all	رَضِيَ اللهُ عَنْهُمْ
7.	*Raḍiyallāhu 'anhā* May Allah be pleased with her	رَضِيَ اللهُ عَنْهَا

Select Bibliography

1. *The Glorious Qur'ān*
2. *al Jāme' al-Ṣaḥīḥ* — Imām Bukhārī
3. *al-Adab al-Mufrad* — Imām Bukhārī
4. *al-Jāme' al-Ṣaḥīḥ* — Imām Muslim
5. *al-Jāme'* — Imām Tirmidhī
6. *al-Sunan* — Imām Abū Dā'ūd
7. *al-Sunan* — Imām Nasā'ī
8. *al-Sunan* — Imām Ibn Mājah
9. *Mishkāt al-Maṣābīḥ* — Waliyyuddīn al-Khaṭīb
10. *Iḥya' 'Ulūm-ad-Dīn* — Imām Ghazālī
11. *Radd al-Muḥtār* — Ibn 'Ābidīn
12. *al-Durr al-Mukhtār* — 'Alā'uddīn al-Ḥaṣkafī
13. *Shamā'il* — Imām Tirmidhī
14. *Al-Musnad* — Imām Aḥmad b. Ḥanbal
15. *Al-Sunan al-Kubrā* — Imām Baihaqī
16. *Shu'ab al-Īmān* — Imām Baihaqī
17. *Jam'-ul-Fawā'id* — Muḥammad b. Sulaimān al-Fāsī
18. *Mufīd al-'Ulūm* — Al-Khawārizmī
19. *Al-Mu'jam al-Awsaṭ* — Imām Tabarānī
20. *Kanz-ul-'Ummāl* — 'Alī Muttaqī Hindī